Handel's Messiah

W9-BJN-945

Joseph E. McCabe

Here the glorious text of Handel's "Messiah" comes alive with new meaning and inspiration. Dr. McCabe interprets each of the twenty-two Bible passages that provide the words to this great work. The twenty-two passages are the ones we most frequently hear sung. The appendix gives additional passages, so that the book includes the complete text of the "Messiah."

Dr. Joseph E. McCabe is President Emeritus, Coe College, Cedar Rapids, Iowa. In the summers he serves as Minister, Saint Timothy Memorial Chapel, Southern Cross, Montana.

HANDEL'S MESSIAH

HANDEL'S MESSIAH

A Devotional Commentary

Joseph E. McCabe

Phoenix Press

WALKER AND COMPANY
New York

Large Print Edition published by arrangement with The Westminster Press

Copyright © 1978 by The Westminster Press

Printed in the United States of America.

Library of Congress Cataloging in Publication Data

McCabe, Joseph E., 1912–
   Handel's Messiah.

   Bibliography: p.
   1. Advent—Prayer-books and devotions—English.
2. Handel, George Frideric, 1685–1759. Messiah.
I. Handel, George Frideric, 1685–1759. Messiah.
II. Title.
BV40.M24 1986   242'.33   86–15053
ISBN 0-8027-2556-2 (lg. print)

First Large Print Edition, 1986
Walker and Company
720 Fifth Avenue
New York, NY 10019

To three of the next generation
        Brandt, Alice, and Tom
and
        To Lois
who has helped so much

Contents

Preface

To Feed the Soul and to Renew the Mind

Advent is the season of expectation. We await the visitation of this wayside planet, for our salvation. No other time of year so focuses our human affection. With Christmas as its climax, Advent is the season for great rejoicing in human loves, and the glad welcome of One who binds us to himself in the love of God.

Later in the Christian year, in Lent, our thoughts are centered on the passion of our Lord, and that is good. But at Advent we are invited to stand back and see the whole life, from his coming forth to his going hence. It is a pageant that, for the sheer drama of it all, has never been surpassed. For us who believe, it is the power of God, in action for our salvation.

That wondrous journey from Bethlehem to the empty tomb, and from the self to God, is all portrayed before us in Handel's *Messiah*. To make that pilgrimage, with the glorious music and the deepest meaning of the familiar words, is to know ourselves to be living in grace. Our souls soar with Handel, while with all our critical powers we plumb the depths of the love of God as set out for us in the Biblical passages.

More than that, *Messiah* is an interpretation of history. Here is the audacious claim that the Author of the whole drama has visited his creation, redemptively. By his coming, each life is crowned with glory. In his death, our sins are dead. And he shall reign—nothing less than that is the goal of the historical process. Personal, yet cosmic, here lie the meaning and the joy.

These glorious solos and choruses, forever wedded and welded now to the Biblical material, have sung themselves into the consciousness of a grateful humanity. As each Advent season comes round again, throughout the world *Messiah* comes to life, a veritable annual resurrection. The secret of its power lies in the depths of the human heart as well as on the pages of the musical score.

The choir of the village church, scarcely a dozen faithful souls in number, can bless the congregation by venturing into the depths of this music. What must it have been to hear the five thousand massed voices at the Crystal Palace, Sydenham, England, just before the First World War, when from that mighty choir arose:

> "And he shall reign for ever and ever.
> King of Kings, and Lord of Lords.
> Hallelujah!"

A Way for the Soul's Growth

Advent begins with the fourth Sunday before Christmas, and continues through Christmas Eve. Thus the season may have as few as twenty-two days and as many as twenty-eight. The familiar *Messiah* text, as most frequently sung in modern times, has been divided, using the lesser number. Each of the twenty-two Biblical passages is printed in full, followed by a devotional commentary. There is one passage for each day, beginning with the first Sunday in Advent and running through the Sunday immediately before Christmas.

Read the text, and as you read, "hear" the music.

Move through the meditation that follows.

Then after reading the meditation, return

once more to the Biblical passage.

Most readers will probably wish to center on one passage daily in Advent. To focus each day on one theme from Scripture, and to grow in the grace it affords, would be an Advent discipline for the soul's good.

Another need may also be met. More and more we are coming to see that longer periods are needed for Bible-reading, contemplation, and prayer. Here is material for a full day's retreat, or an even longer period, when one can read, walk, meditate, and pray.

The poorest use of all would be simply to read page after page, without taking time for that inward renewal which comes to those who wait patiently in Advent.

The written meditation should prompt devotional reflection, not exhaust it. Let the commentary be a thought starter for the day, an invitation to pilgrimage. Return again and again to the Bible passage. There is where the devotional life is to be grounded, not in the commentary.

The language of devotion is borrowed language. In our prayers we employ the phrases and thoughts of the centuries. These meditations borrow words and expressions not my own, but whose parentage is lost forever to me.

It is in devotional language particularly that we are indebted to all who have inspired and blessed us. Who can measure such obligation? All claims to originality are pretentious. One remembers authors and books with gratitude, even when the particular source is elusive. Perhaps we are most indebted in the language of the soul to those who have joined the more active side of the communion of saints.

An Obscure Appendix, Where Some Light Is

If there yet remain any days before Christmas after the most familiar part of *Messiah* has been covered, the material in the Appendixes may prove helpful. Some of it may appear clouded and of little spiritual help. Sir Thomas Beecham says of the music for these passages: "It has always been and still is the opinion of the great majority of practicing musicians that these are not only on a lower inspirational level than the rest of the work, but halt its admirably rapid pace and dramatic continuity." Though seldom heard now, these passages are set forth here to maintain the complete text of *Messiah* as employed by Handel and as originally performed.

Yet in obscurity, light arises. "Death is swallowed up in victory." Who would want to lose that? But: "The Lord gave the word: great was the company of the preachers." Even the ordained among us could not quarrel with its omission.

The original work and first performance closed with: "If God be for us, who can be against us?" This ringing affirmation is no longer heard in *Messiah*, simply because the music does not match the text in the collective judgment of those best fitted to decide.

Grateful Tribute to the Composer

The longtime and greatly beloved conductor of the London Symphony Orchestra, Sir Thomas Beecham, writes of Handel in his memoirs: "Since his time mankind has heard no music written for voices which can even feebly rival his for grandeur of build and tone, nobility and tenderness of melody, scholastic skill and ingenuity and inexhaustible variety of effect." A multitude that no man can number would bear testimony to Beecham's verdict.

Messiah has been a wondrous blessing for more than two centuries. That will prove to be a good beginning as future generations hear the work with thanksgiving. When Biblical truth is joined to music that reaches the soul, then the human spirit soars. May it be so with *Messiah* lovers for years to come.

Cosmic in scope, yet deeply personal in its appeal, this artistic triumph points beyond our little day, for "the Lord God omnipotent reigneth." That will be for eternity.

Most of Handel's busy life was concerned with secular music, but it is clearly this work which is best remembered. Even so, may our little lives be redeemed by the Eternal, who meets us here in *Messiah*.

JOSEPH E. McCABE

Advent, 1977

Handel's Messiah:

A Devotional Commentary

1

Comfort ye, comfort ye my people, saith your God; speak ye comfortably to Jerusalem; and cry unto her, that her warfare is accomplished, that her iniquity is pardoned.

The voice of him that crieth in the wilderness, Prepare ye the way of the Lord, make straight in the desert a highway for our God.

COMFORT ye—what a good word to the human heart from the heart of God. That first word is the best word. To know that the Creator is also the comforter is to have peace at the center. Behind the cosmos is One who cares. He who knows all is he who loves most. You are known completely. And you are loved eternally. Therefore: "Comfort ye."

There are other words from God to us. They, like this first word, are authentic. The other words will speak of obedience, discipleship, and judgment. Some of them are hard to hear, and harder yet to obey. In all honesty, could we expect the One who knows us fully to comfort us only? That would not be kind, for we know in our hearts that to gloss over our infection would be to leave us as we are, and as we are we are not whole.

Just because our need is great there will be words of challenge and rebuke, stringent surgery for our healing. We may not welcome those other words, but we will surely meet them on this spiritual journey.

But the first word is: "Comfort ye." Amid our crushing burdens, and those gnawing anxieties which torment so terribly, it speaks to us. Right beside the suffering we endure, which might drive out the saving trust, there stands the word to lift up our hearts: "Comfort ye." For our iniquity is pardoned. That is the news beautiful which breaks upon us in Advent.

INTO the wilderness of our hearts, and into the desert of our despair, someone is coming. Where he comes, and where he is received, there comes also the high calling to make straight in all the deserts of the world a highway for our God. He lays that task upon us. He who comforts us is he who thrusts us into the desert, for kingdom-building. That old language simply means that we who are forgiven are charged to forge a social order to the liking of God.

Cheap comfort is all around us. The old fakers and soothsayers still abound. They come now in glossy print and popular pulpits. We are to let the sweet fragrance engulf us, even as we read the next chapter, or hear the same sweet sermon next Sunday. They offer us the comforting assurance that we are really quite respectable, and that the tiger in our hearts is tame.

He who speaks to us in Advent knows better. He knows the wilderness into which we have wandered, and the wildness of the world we have on our hands. It is precisely

5

there we are to prepare the way of the Lord. Into the desert of this weary world we are thrust to transform and make it blossom and rejoice. That is the call. He lays that task upon us. We avoid it at the peril of missing life's most important appointment.

The comfort and the call—these are the two sides of our high faith. What God has joined together, we separate at our soul's peril.

YET that imperious call, the noble task appointed, is not the first word in Advent. That would send us forth once more in our own strength, to meet defeat once more. The first word is from the loving power behind the universe, the power that moves the stars and knows your name.

"Comfort ye." That is the first word and the best. If we will receive that word in the depths of our being, we can face anything. But do not try to face the world again alone. Do not try grasping God. That is as fragile as the other things you grasp.

> "Let me no more my comfort draw
>   From my frail hold on thee,
> In this alone rejoice with awe,
>   Thy mighty grasp of me."

Today we begin the Advent journey, especially the journey of the soul toward God. We begin, not at Bethlehem, but in the mind of God, where all beginnings are. After a prologue, we are to witness a birth, knowing that through the world's folly there is to be a black afternoon outside a city wall.

The hands that reached up to his mother's face as a little child are the hands that will be pierced. We are to view the entire life in this Advent season, from the cradle to the cross, and beyond.

The first word as we begin the pilgrimage is: "Comfort ye."

Scripture leads us to believe that it is the word we shall hear again when, trembling, we come into God's presence at last.

2

AIR [TENOR]

Every valley shall be exalted, and every mountain and hill made low; the crooked straight, and the rough places plain.

CHORUS

And the glory of the Lord shall be revealed, and all flesh shall see it together; for the mouth of the Lord hath spoken it.

WHAT a preposterous claim! "The crooked straight, and the rough places plain"—in a world like ours?

We were once so hopeful. The vision and the dream we once held for a suffering humanity was part of the high idealism of our youth, and the youth of our culture. We saw life working upward through evolution, and concluded all social institutions were like that, steadily moving upward toward a better world. Surely all humanity would soon embrace our form of government, our economic system, and our faith.

Perhaps our despair is so deep just because we have fallen so far from that high hope. Life was to be fair, in a world both safe and just. In the days of our youth we may have believed it, but now we know better. The crooked ways in the world, and the rough places, have so assaulted us that the great expectation has fled, even from our dreams.

No, we do not know better. We know

worse, and have accepted the worst of our day as the permanent condition of the world. We have embraced the pessimism and breathed deeply of the gloom, as though that were our native air. Having lost the dream of youth, we have embraced a greater foolishness, the belief that all there is, is all there is to be.

Advent brings the bracing word to high faith once more. That faith comes like a cool wind from snowcapped peaks, cleansing the atmosphere for our souls. The crooked shall be made straight and the rough places shall be made plain. That is not a blueprint, but a certainty. There is no timetable, for all times are in God's hands. It is a promise, sealed with Advent reality.

OUR task is not to be great, which has eluded us, but to be faithful. To *believe* greatly, and to work at it with fidelty, that is the commission laid upon us now. It is better than the dreams of our youth, for then history was to be consummated by our efforts. What pride was there! Now we know history is to be consummated by God, and not by us. We are to be faithful.

Over a tortuous mountain pass a group of day laborers were felling trees and moving boulders. That is a pretty menial job. They and the chief engineer knew a road would surely follow, whether they ever saw it or not. Just so, we are to work, in faith.

"All flesh shall see it together." That is not my little group alone, or my great church only, or my beloved country, but all. You cannot feel sure any longer that anyone is excluded. You cannot trust God to shut anyone out. Parochialism is gone. He has wrapped the banner of his love around our exclusions with a word: "all flesh."

What is our confidence? Our strong hands, and our cleverness, shall they bring to pass the great desire? No. "The mouth of the Lord hath spoken it." That is the rock on which to stand. It is not the work of our hands, but the word of our God which stands forever. You are invited in Advent to trust that word.

READ the text again before you read on. . . . You do think at once about the need for world order, improved race relations, and all the other problems of our plagued humanity.

What about the crooked in your own life, and those rough places which make you so difficult to live with at times?

"As I prepare within myself a way
    For thy pure feet to walk my desert
    soul,
How many crooked places must be
    straightened,
    How many weak and broken things
    made whole!"

The promise and the power is for each struggling soul. Old habits still grip, and we show our rough places even to those we love. How escape? Do you simply will to do better, and to be finer? You have been willing it for a long time.

When habit and will are in conflict, habit

wins every time. Not by resolution chiefly does inner change come, but by a steady gaze at him who comes at Advent. He comes with transforming power to the soul that looks steadily at him, and not at the self.

"Look unto him, all the ends of the earth." That is the far reach of the promise. But the soul needs most of all to stand back and behold his coming. And as you meditate upon the wonder of it all, you will be changed, even a little, into his likeness.

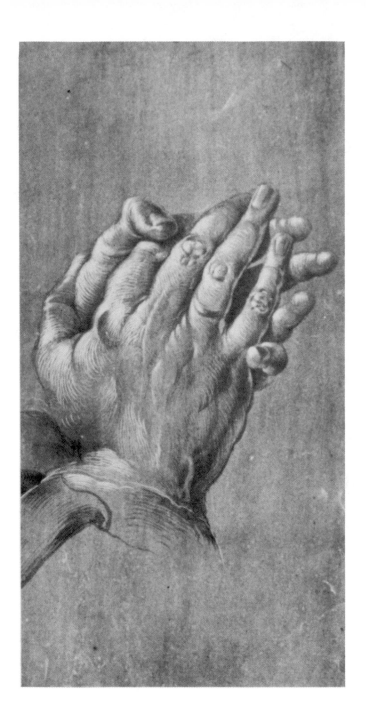

3

RECITATIVE [BASS]   ACCOMPANIED

Thus saith the Lord of Hosts: Yet once a little while and I will shake the heavens and the earth, the sea and the dry land; and I will shake all nations; and the desire of all nations shall come. The Lord, whom ye seek, shall suddenly come to his temple, even the messenger of the covenant, whom ye delight in; Behold, he shall come, saith the Lord of Hosts.

AIR [BASS]

But who may abide the day of his coming, and who shall stand when he appeareth? For he is like a refiner's fire.

CHORUS

And he shall purify the sons of Levi, that they may offer unto the Lord an offering in righteousness.

THE judgment of God is inherent in the love of God. How so? He loves you too much to allow you to continue in ways that are not for your good. You chastise a little child for running into the street. That is judgment, for love's sake. How much more does your heavenly Father love you.

William Temple wrote: "For very love's sake God will be relentlessly stern against all in us that is self-centered; our lower nature and unconverted hearts are likely often to think Him cruel. . . . The love of God is not a sentimental readiness to give us what we happen to want; it is a passionate yearning to raise us to its own likeness."

A young woman told the minister all her sins, and they were many. "You must think me a pretty poor Christian," she concluded. "That would be passing judgment," he replied, and then, "Haven't you had judgment already?" "Yes," she said softly, "I have had to live with that every day." It was judgment that brought her back

to church, back to Christ, and to a glad
fresh beginning. It was judgment unto
life.

GOD'S will for you is that you be the best person possible. When you are less than your best, God is wounded, and you have little joy. His passing of judgment is for the purpose of restoring you to your true value, your best self. If he were not a God of judgment, he would not be a God of love. For love wills that you turn to the light, and woos you with love until you do so.

The judgment of God is not anger. It is what authentic love always does. God's judgment is love in action appropriate to the situation. Scripture says: "If I make my bed in hell, behold, thou art there." Love follows even to the lowest, and judges, in order that we may be restored again to the heights. It is judgment unto life. He comes in judgment, and he does shake us, indeed he does, for love's sake.

God also shakes the nations. Lincoln saw it clearly, and wrote in his Second Inaugural Address: "The Almighty has his own purposes. . . . If we shall suppose that American slavery is one of those offenses which, in the providence of God, must needs come, but which, having continued through His appointed time, He now wills to remove, and that He gives to both North and South this terrible war as the woe due to those by whom the offense came, shall we discern therein any departure from those divine attributes which the believers in a living God always ascribe to Him?" The nation was being shaken, and Lincoln was saying the war was not a judgment thrown down from a vindictive infinity, but the natural working out of the moral law which is applicable to nations as well as to individuals.

A century after lincoln we saw judgment upon nations again. America sold scrap iron to Japan for that nation to fight China, and a few years later it was exploding among our own troops in the South Pacific. Germany's Reich drove out Jewish scientists who then helped the Allies develop weapons to defeat their persecutors. There is judgment in history.

Return to the personal. Doesn't it shake you to know, in the words of the old prayer, that your heart is open to God, your desires known to him, and the deepest secret of your life is not hid from him?

When that truth grasps you, then you understand that strange question in *Messiah* about who may abide the day of his coming, and who shall stand when he appears. The old spiritual has truth: "Everybody talkin' 'bout heaven ain't going there." You know now that not everyone who says "Lord, Lord" shall enter the kingdom.

He who comes at Advent is he who shall purify the sons of Levi. Take your place with those sons, for your need qualifies you. Pray that the refiner's fire shall consume all that would separate you from him who is coming. That would be judgment unto life.

"Behold, he shall come." He shall come in these expectant days to those whose longing is to be purified. From the depths of this longing, pray the last words of the Bible: "Even so, come, Lord Jesus."

4

RECITATIVE [CONTRALTO]

Behold, a virgin shall conceive and bear a Son, and shall call his name Emmanuel, God with us.

EMMANUEL, God with us. If that were lacking, who could go on? Because it is true, anything can be endured, with a certain trace of triumph. Other things are most desirable, things like food and drink and clothing, and the precious people we love. But what if you had them all, yet felt God eternally absent? There is a hunger in the human heart which will be satisfied with nothing less than that creative love behind the universe, named God. Advent is the comingness of God.

"He has given us the sun and the moon and the stars, the earth with its forests and mountains and oceans and all that lives and moves upon them. He has given us all green things and everything that blossoms and bears fruit—and all that we quarrel about and that we have misused. And to save us from our own foolishnesses and from all our sins He came down to Earth and gave Himself. *Venite adoremus Dominum.*" O come let us adore him.

Never again are we to look at the stars as

we did when we were children, and wonder how far it is to God. A being outside our world would be a spectator, looking on but taking no part in this life where we try to be brave despite all the bafflement. A God who created, and withdrew, could be mighty, but he could not be love. Who could love a God remote when suffering is our lot? Our God is closer than our problems, for they are out there, to be faced. He is here, beside us, Emmanuel.

WHY didn't this meditation begin with the first words of the passage? "Behold, a virgin shall conceive and bear a Son." We began with the nature of God, to be with his people. Was he not with them before Jesus came? Of course he was. There is a parody on the third chapter of Exodus incident:

"Earth's crammed with heaven,
And every common bush afire with God,
But only he who sees takes off his shoes,
Others just stand round and pick the
      blackberries."

God is, and always has been, everywhere. His coming in Jesus of Nazareth is the miracle supreme. God is eternally all that we see in Jesus Christ.

Virgin birth? Yes, we must be willing to let God be God, if that's the way he came. To say he could not come that way is the same as saying he is not God. A person who believes in the virgin birth should cherish that belief, and thank God that he has it.

What if you do not believe in the virgin birth, or what if you commute between belief and doubt? Be of good cheer. No one was ever saved by the virgin birth of Jesus. You are saved by him who was born. Take your stand with Peter and Paul, who at their conversion had never heard of the virgin birth. They were wondrously saved.

The doctrine of the virgin birth points to a purity we have not known, to that dedication of Mary's to which we have not attained, and to the courage of Joseph we have not matched. Never scorn such virtue and such selflessness.

Christ saves. He may or may not bring you to belief in his virgin birth. But if you are his, he has already done more. He has brought you to belief in himself, and that is salvation.

AGAIN, "Emmanuel, God with us." In all our plans and confusion, amid our dreams and our dread, our hope and our hopelessness, he is with us? Yes, that is Advent reality. An emperor said to his followers, "I cannot spare you the battle, but I can eat your black bread and lie with you on the hard ground." How much more —God. He is not a God who spares us the battle. He is our God who is in it with us, all the way.

God is he from whom you are never apart. Your awareness of him may dim, but not his awareness of you. Every believer has had the experience of Augustine: "Thou wast with me, O God, but I was not with Thee." There is a veil of flesh, until we see God face to face. In willfullness we may turn back, in pain we may be blinded with both grief and tears so that we cannot see, and by the power of reason we may doubt reason's Source. None of these changes the fact of the whereabouts of God. He is here.

The Advent hymn "O come, O come,

Emmanuel" is taken from this passage of *Messiah*. He did come, and he comes now. He does not batter down your will if you will to remain apart. He will accept your invitation if you really mean to say: "O come, O come, Emmanuel."

He came. He comes. He remains. Here is his solemn promise to the soul: "Lo, I am with you alway, even unto the end of the world." He who came at Advent said that. Believe, and live forever in his presence.

5

O thou that tellest good tidings to Zion, get thee up into the high mountain: O thou that tellest good tidings to Jerusalem, lift up thy voice with strength; lift it up, be not afraid; say unto the cities of Judah, Behold your God!

Arise, shine, for thy light is come, and the glory of the Lord is risen upon thee.

THY light is come. Advent is good news for the mind. We grope amid a million stars for meaning. We ponder aeons of history, seeking a pattern. Beneath our surface sophistication we long for some ultimate. Are the days of our years flying furiously, nowhere? Are we but ciphers, with the rim rubbed off? The questioning mind cries out for meaning in the whole cosmic process. T. S. Eliot reflects the Advent answer:

"A moment not out of time, but in time, in what we call history: transecting, bisecting the world of time, a moment in time but not like a moment of time.

"A moment in time but time was made through that moment: for without the meaning there is no time, and that moment of time gave the meaning."

We must be rigorous about loving the Lord our God with all our mind. Why? Jesus commanded it. True, we will not be saved by our intellectuality. But our intellects are to be saved from meaninglessness. What a deliverance! The rational is also redeemed. "Lift up your hearts." That is a true call to worship. Lift up your head also. That is Christian obedience.

"O God, I offer thee my heart—
    In many a mystic mood, by beauty led,
I give my heart to thee. But now impart
    That sterner grace—to offer thee my
    head."

THE passage opens with the prophet's admonition to tell good news. For Isaiah it was a hope. For us it is a present reality. Therefore, "Lift up thy voice with strength." Or, as an old Scripture has it, "Let the redeemed of the Lord say so." If we are not moved to shout in the corridors of the Lord, at least let there be whispered praise in the depths of our own being.

It is clear that we are to make our witness. Some will say in the streets: "Jesus saves, and he wants to save you." That is good, and true. Others will be more like Saint Francis. He invited a young follower to go and preach with him. They walked serenely in the crowded streets, greeted all people with a word of cheer, traversed the entire city thusly, and returned to the monastery. The young man, baffled, protested that he had been invited to preach with the saint. "We preached as we walked," was the quiet reply.

A friend's Christmas letter describes the

totalitarian state and the brutalized life under Caesar. He suggests that first-century Christians might have said, "Look what the world has come to." Instead they cried, "Look what has come to the world."

There *is* a witness to be made. Some Christians seem to do it in a way that offends. That is better than the way many Christians do not do it. "Lift up thy voice with strength." At least, lift up thy voice, some way, some time, some place. There is a silence that is creative, and there is a silence that is cowardice. Seek to know the difference.

THE Light that came at Advent is the solvent word for our darkest perplexities. Christ does not take away our problems. He illumines our pathway, and walks it with us. We want to know that there is a reason for it all, a meaning to the process.

"Light of the world
Undimming and unsetting,
O shine each mist away."

If you cannot say, "Christ is my Saviour," at least say, "In him life makes sense." To be saved is better than to know, but the mind is to praise him also. With all our Christmas giving, we might give him our rational powers, and our sharply honed thinking. The source of all truth has come into the world in order that the mind may find a resting-place as well as the heart. Therefore, "It is a duty we owe to God . . . to have our minds constantly disposed to entertain and receive truth wheresoever we meet with it. Our first and great duty is to bring to our studies and to our inquiries after knowledge a mind covetous of truth."

The Scripture passage points to the light, and calls for a witness to the light. We may have come up from the slime after several billion years of creative evolution, but our new status is that the Light has come down from the immeasurable reaches of unimaginable spaces. "Behold the glory of God in the face of Jesus Christ."

Hold to that truth. You may doubt all else, but the single fact of him who came can grip, and sustain, and save. Give him back the gift splendid, your mind. That Light will go on shining in the darkness, and the darkness will never dim its luster.

You now know the central truth of the universe. You can trust him who is the light. Therefore, "arise, shine, for the glory of the Lord is risen upon thee."

6

For, behold, darkness shall cover the earth, and gross darkness the people; but the Lord shall arise upon thee, and his glory shall be seen upon thee, and the Gentiles shall come to thy light, and kings to the brightness of thy rising.

THE struggle between darkness and light is the history of the world. That is good philosophy. The real struggle is between man's darkness and the commandments of God. That is religion. Then came the Advent of Jesus Christ, the Light of the World. That is Christianity.

"Darkness shall cover the earth, and gross darkness the people." Who needs one more dreary cataloging of the world's ills? From your door to the end of the earth and back, the spirit faints. Amid the desolation, we have joined the cry at the slaughter of the innocents in Bethlehem, for many of our dreams have died: "Wailing and loud lamentation, Rachel weeping for her children; and refused to be comforted." The heavy gloom in our day is best described by the words of Exodus as "darkness which may be felt."

There is a world in darkness, and there always has been. Sometimes in the history of the race it has been slightly shadowy. At other times it is all midnight. This whirling planet has never known a day without oppression and hunger. The cynic says that on any clear day the view is terrible. It has always been so. Some days are less dark than others. There is a tragic theme in the human story, made more visible in our day, for indeed the horror has been heightened and is brought daily into the living room.

"Darkness shall cover the earth." That future has become present tense. But in darkness, light arises. In the darkness of Egypt—Moses. In the darkness of Babylon —Isaiah. In the darkness of the Roman Empire—Augustine. In the darkness of the Dark Ages—Aquinas. In the darkness of slavery—Lincoln. In this our day of darkness, God is raising up his prophets, if we have ears to hear, and the will to do what we must, for God and humanity's sake.

DARKNESS can be very personal. If anyone persists in insisting that the glory cannot come to earth, that persistence is respected by God. Frozen unbelief may plead: "Come not in darkness, come not in light," for some changes would have to be made. The change from confident unbelief can be painful before it is blessing. Ptolemaic astronomy made the earth the centre of the universe, and thus all its conclusions were wrong. When anything or any person other than Jesus Christ is made the center of the universe, or the center of the church, or the center of one's life, God's order of reality is missed.

Scripture holds that men prefer darkness rather than light because their deeds are evil. True, but often we do not prefer darkness. We just find the light too good to be true. An American told an Oriental that back in his country it gets so cold in winter he can walk on the water. The Oriental resolved right then and there never to talk with so demented a tourist again. That is quaint and costless ignorance. But consider the terrible words of the New Testament: "If the light that is in you be darkness, how great is that darkness!"

"Gentiles shall come to thy light, and kings to the brightness of thy rising." That is ablaze with expectation. We are not known for our rapture, precisely because we have not embraced the revelation. Rapture escapes us because the revelation does not fit our rational categories. We want final truth to be in a syllogism, or a test tube, or at the farthest telescopic view of outer space. What we are given is a Face, born of a woman, under these ordinary skies.

IT is in the school of darkness where we learn to love the light. Was it not in darkness and suffering that we learned to climb at last:

"... the great world's altar-stairs
That slope thro' darkness up to God."

In the old language of Clement of Alexandria, written many centuries ago, early Christians are described as "holding festival . . . in our whole life, persuaded that God is altogether on every side present, we cultivate our fields, praising; we sail the sea, hymning."

The mighty aircraft carrier was sailing through heavy seas in the South Pacific. Night came, but one plane was still up there somewhere, searching for the ship, its only landing place. Enemy submarines were also in the area. Any light abroad was forbidden. Only the captain could give the order, which he did: "Light up the ship." At what terrible risk the missing was saved. Even so, Christ came, the Light, at what risk.

"Darkness shall cover the earth, and gross darkness the people." That is present fact and persistent history. In Advent there is Light.

"That one Face, far from vanish, rather
    grows,
Or decomposes but to recompose,
Become my universe that feels and
    knows."

7

AIR [BASS]

The people that walked in darkness have seen a great light; and they that dwell in the land of the shadow of death, upon them hath the light shined.

CHORUS

For unto us a Child is born, unto us a Son is given, and the government shall be upon his shoulder; and his name shall be called Wonderful, Counsellor, the Mighty God, the Everlasting Father, the Prince of Peace.

THEY that dwell in the land of the shadow of death, upon them hath the light shined. What was that Roman land like? We are always tempted to think of the fine roads, aqueducts so architecturally pleasing, philosopher-senators, and the finest system of law yet known. There is abroad a nostalgia for a time that never was, as though the law and order of those days were worth the inconvenience of dictatorship. What was that Roman land really like? It takes one from a shadowed land to tell us. So Pasternak writes:

"Rome was a flea market of borrowed gods and conquered peoples, a bargain basement on two floors, earth and heaven, a mass of filth convoluted in a triple knot as in an intestinal obstruction.

"Dacians, Herulians, Scythians, Sarmatians, Hyperboreans, heavy wheels without spokes, eyes sunk in fat, sodomy, double chins, illiterate emperors, fish fed on the flesh of learned slaves . . . all crammed in-

51

to the passages of the Coliseum, and all wretched.

"And then, into this tasteless heap of gold and marble, He came, light and clothed in an aura, emphatically human, deliberately provincial, Galilean, and at that moment gods and nations ceased to be and man came into being—

"Man the carpenter, man the plowman, man the shepherd with his flock of sheep at sunset, man who does not sound in the least proud, man thankfully celebrated in all the cradle songs of mothers and in all the picture galleries of the world over."

THERE are countries today where the human spirit dwells "in the land of the shadow." Freedom, dignity, choice—these have been stripped from millions. Scripture is fulfilled: "The whole land grieves."

Yet in every country under heaven there are those who praise God that the light of Advent has come. Under the Caesars, Christians gathered underground, and in caves of the earth, to whisper: "Christus, Christus." So in our day, from prisons and from exile, the human spirit dwells in the shadow, but upon them the Light shines. "A bruised reed, he will not break, and the smoldering flax, he will not extinguish." Thanks be to God for his faithfulness in the lands of the shadow.

Biologically now, and personally, we are all dwellers in the land of the shadow of *death*. That is a great blessing. What if everyone on earth were to live forever on this earth? Hell would be tame compared with that chaos. Morning and evening, spring and fall, birthing and departing—those are built-in blessings from within a benevolent creation. Christ, being born of a woman, was destined to die, and so are we. Be grateful for that providential destiny. It is of course the last appointment on the way to life. Therefore, rejoice, all who were born to die. "For unto us a Child is born, unto us a Son is given."

ARE we now all in shadow until the Lord comes—rather, until we come to him? If you had been born in a basement without windows, and lived there all your life, the only light a fifteen-watt bulb, how could you know about a brighter light, a fairer world? We need to be taken out from all little lights, grateful as we are for them, and stand free in the sunshine. Do not plead to be able to look directly into the sun, just live by its light, with thanksgiving. Shine upon us, O Light of the World, whether we see thee or not.

The chorus from *Messiah* touches this passage with grandeur. There is majestic cadence, as though a host were marching straight up the mountain: "And the government shall be upon his shoulder." Then comes the crashing climax: "Wonderful, Counsellor, the Might God, the Everlasting Father, the Prince of Peace." As musical artistry for human voices it has never been surpassed. As providential promise it is unmatched among all the hopes of humanity.

"The ultimate truth," said William Temple, "is not a system of propositions grasped by a perfect intelligence, but is a Personal Being apprehended by love." A child he was once, flesh of our flesh, and a Son forever.

Despite all shadows over all lands, or over our lives, God has set a hunger in our hearts for him who was born at Bethlehem. In Advent, let us journey thither. It may mean:

"Only the road and the dawn, the sun, the wind, and the rain,
And the watch fire under stars, and sleep, and the road again."

You may not find a city at all, but you will find a Saviour. When you meet Jesus Christ you will say, "Isaiah's tumultuous words never told us even half of it."

8

RECITATIVE [SOPRANO]

There were shepherds abiding in the field, keeping watch over their flocks by night.

RECITATIVE [SOPRANO]   ACCOMPANIED

And lo, the angel of the Lord came upon them, and the glory of the Lord shone round about them, and they were sore afraid.

RECITATIVE [SOPRANO]

And the angel said unto them, Fear not; for, behold, I bring you good tidings of great joy, which shall be to all people. For unto you is born this day in the city of David a Saviour, which is Christ the Lord.

SOME things have changed but little in two thousand years. You can still walk through the fields east of Bethlehem. The olive orchards there still hold gray loveliness. Sheep wander through the fields, and among the trees, looking up only to measure the distance to the leaves, then turn back to the hard ground, where grass is sparse. Gray-haired shepherds are still there in the fields, each with a crook in his hand, and at twilight they bring the sheep to the fold. Beyond the fields, as evening comes on, the lights come on in Bethlehem. It is all so much like any field, any town, anywhere. Not much has changed.

"And they were sore afraid." Has that changed? Only in this way—the fear is even sorer now, there in the land of Christ's birth, and here in our land, and in every land under the Advent skies. Fear is now every person's portion, near Bethlehem, near your door, and within both. Not much has changed.

So many voices have told us not to fear. The wise counselor says so to quiet us, and the ignorant vigilante says so, for he can handle anything. One political leader says fear is all we need to fear, while another statesman hopes to allay our fears by saying mutual fear will deal with the ultimate fear. Thus many voices try, some sincerely, some bravely, some with great courage, but underneath them all we detect something akin to our own voice, and it is fearful.

The heart longs for a voice other than its own, in which it will not disbelieve. That voice was heard at the First Advent. "Fear not . . . good tidings . . . great joy." That voice is speaking still. Not much has changed.

SOME fear is good. Fear of natural fire is sane. How much more should we fear failure to be God's person. Some people deeply fear faith, for faith would call for change, which is painful. Jesus said: "I have come to cast fire on the earth." Do not fear that fire, for it scorches, cauterizes, and deeply heals. Fear natural fire, but be warmed and purified by the Advent fire, without which life is not only cold but fearful.

"Fear not." How those simple words gather up the Biblical material for our strengthening. If we begin with an ancient psalm, there it is written: "I sought the Lord, and he heard me, and delivered me from all my fears." If we go to Bethlehem's child, grown to maturity, we hear him say in manhood: "Why are you so fearful? How is it that you have no faith?"

A person who has Biblical faith can walk and work without fear. Are these the worst of times? Only for those for whom life has no living Lord. How are we to live? Faithfully, and without paralyzing fear. In the heart of England there stands a chapel bearing this inscription:

IN THE YEAR 1653
WHEN ALL THINGS SACRED WERE
THROUGHOUT THE NATION
EITHER DEMOLISHED OR PROFANED
SIR ROBERT SHIRLEY BARONET
FOUNDED THIS CHURCH
WHOSE SINGULAR PRAISE IT IS
TO HAVE DONE THE BEST THINGS
IN THE WORST TIMES
AND
HOPED THEM IN THE MOST CALAMITOUS

IN the city of David a Saviour. It is the city of the heart's desire. All cities of man will perish. They belong to the order of things that change. There is the historical city of Bethlehem, which changes, and which will ultimately perish. But there is also the city of the heart's desire, our private Bethlehem where the Saviour is born, again and again, at Advent. Journey with wise men to that Bethlehem within.

"To an open house in the evening
Home shall men come,
To an older place than Eden
And a taller town than Rome.
To the end of the way of the wandering
    star,
To the things that cannot be and that are,
To the place where God was homeless
And all men are at home."

Our faith is anchored in history. In a particular place, a dusty wayside village, an Eastern place of little reckoning by man's measurement, there Christ the Lord was born. It is not a wild hope thrown up against the winter sky, but a real event. A historical happening is the center of our hopes. In Bethlehem, Christ was born. The world has never been the same. "Where God was homeless and all men are at home." If your heart is home for him, then he is not homeless, and you need fear no more.

9

And suddenly there was with the angel a multitude of the heavenly host, praising God, and saying:

CHORUS

Glory to God in the highest, and peace on earth, good will towards men.

THIS *Messiah* passage describes authentic worship, for the angels were praising God, not taking their own spiritual pulse. "Glory to God in the highest." When a person says that from the heart, anything may happen. Worship centers the soul in God and is a turning from self to life's true source and center.

Beware of true worship. It may lead you from yourself to God. What a pilgrimage that can be, and shaking to the soul. In worship you will see that God does love you, and the Russians, and the butcher, and the Chinese, and all members of the opposite political party, and Communists. It is in worship you may come to understand that quite clearly, and, wonder upon wonder, you may feel it deeply. Religious imperialism is gone from our culture—thank God. We point to Jesus Christ, but we compel no one. When we simply point to Christ, he draws people to himself. The New Testament bids us believe he wants them on no other basis.

What truth there is in Buddhism, and what real good there is in Hinduism, are all from the one source—God. Do not deny any person's truth; rather, point to the One who is the source of all truth. Peace on earth is just like truth, it is for all. Did the angels sing: "Glory to God in the highest, and peace to my country and my church"? That would have been one more dreary episode in our perpetual self-centeredness. Advent is the antidote to our egocentricity.

"Gather us in, thou Love that fillest all!
    Gather our rival faiths within thy fold.
Rend each man's temple veil and bid it
            fall,
    That we may know that thou hast been
            of old;
        Gather us in."

TRY thinking Christ is only for you. You can't. Try thinking Christ is only for your church. You can't. Try thinking God wants peace only for your nation. . . . Better quit thinking about God, and Christ, and peace, for it is terribly disturbing. But at the end of the disturbance you may see: "He's got the whole world in his hands."

God was giving at that First Advent. "God so loved the world that he gave . . ." The New Testament does not say God so loved the church, or God so loved our nation. He does love both. He loves both church and nation for the world's sake. The church and the nation are to be instruments of his peace, for the whole world.

Once it was every caveman for himself. Then came the cave family, blessed addition, and the caveman was better for it. Then came the tribe, and the family was better for its coming. Then came the nation, and all tribes were strengthened by its coming. Shall we not say someday: "Then came humanity, and all nations were blessed for its coming"?

All calls for world peace go to pieces on the self-centeredness of individuals or nations. The rock of national sovereignty has been a blessing. It may prove to be the final obstacle to peace on earth. No nation should give away its sovereignty. Every nation must learn to share sovereignty, to spend a little sovereignty, for humanity's sake.

GLORY to God. In *Messiah* the chorus sings it over and over. Let it sing in your heart, and sink into the depths of your being. It is when you sing, "Glory to God in the highest," that life on earth is good. When one does not sing of glory to God, he may fall into that utter foolishness in which Swinburne sang:

"Thou art smitten, thou God, thou art smitten;
    thy death is upon thee, O Lord.
And the love-song of earth as thou diest resounds
    through the wind of her wings—
Glory to Man in the highest! for Man is
    the master of things."

Such pride now lies shattered. May it be gone forever. In place of foolish pride, Advent offers us the peace of God. Instead of man, the master of things, we worship God, maker of all things, and giver of peace. The ancient Scripture points to our final trust:

"For the mountains shall depart, and the hills be removed; but thy kindness shall not depart from me, neither shall the covenant of thy peace be removed."

The peace of God is personal peace. It is deeply and wonderfully personal. God's peace is for you this Advent. He loves you as much as though there were just one in all the universe to be loved. Let that peace flood your heart. Let that peace come over your troubled mind. That is the peace which the Bible describes as the peace which the world cannot give, and which the world can never take away. It is God's peace, for you.

10

AIR [SOPRANO]

Rejoice greatly, O daughter of Zion! Shout, O daughter of Jerusalem! Behold, thy King cometh unto thee. He is the righteous Saviour, and he shall speak peace unto the heathen.

RECITATIVE [CONTRALTO]

Then shall the eyes of the blind be opened, and the ears of the deaf unstopped; then shall the lame man leap as a hart, and the tongue of the dumb shall sing.

REJOICE greatly—so Scripture admonishes us in Advent. We seek our joy in so many things whose pleasure is passing. We rejoice over friends and food, loved ones and leisure, and so many good things. Why, then, is there not more lasting joy in the depths of our lives?

It is right that we should rejoice in all the good gifts of life. Spiritual danger arises when we possess them as by right, and when we forget that they are made possible by a providential creation. "What hast thou that thou didst not receive?" That Scripture convicts us. The self-made man is always in danger of worshiping his creator.

Spiritual health is to enjoy the good things that we possess, to recognize their transient nature, and to rejoice that our lives are rooted and grounded in the Eternal. There are some people so dependent upon their possessions that if they were taken away, the whole personality would be shattered. Others live with such a lively sense of Providence that if all possessions were suddenly to disappear, the center and strength of the soul would still hold fast.

In Advent we are admonished not only to rejoice but to shout. Some Christians simply live an underkeyed life, and a sanctified shout would appear unseemly. Of course it is an attitude of the soul, and not some form of verbalizing, that is at issue.

We are to rejoice and shout in Advent, not because of the abundance of our possessions, but because a king is coming. The world is not much impressed nowadays by earthly kings, for all have feet of clay. But this king is the righteous Saviour, and he shall speak peace unto what is still the heathen in our hearts. For the coming of a king who can do that, let us praise God, yes, even shout for joy.

IT is a plaintive and lovely musical line to which the contralto sings of blind eyes being opened and deaf ears being unstopped. The lame man shall leap and the tongue that has never spoken shall sing. Text and music combine to set forth a loveliness emerging from life's unspeakable tragedies.

It was this very passage Jesus had in mind when he sent his message to John in prison. From his cell, John had forwarded the crucial question to Christ: "Are you he who is to come, or shall we look for another?" There is the deepest cry of the human heart. Jesus replied: "Go and tell John what you hear and see: the blind receive their sight and the lame walk, lepers are cleansed and the deaf hear, and the dead are raised upon and the poor have good news preached to them." Having sent this message to John, whose whole life was faithfulness, Jesus set out faithfully to fulfill all he had said of himself.

And it all happened. When this righteous Saviour walked the streets and countryside of Palestine, both the vision of the prophet and his own words became reality. One man said openly: "Whereas I was blind, now I see." Another took up his bed and walked. No doubt he felt like leaping for joy. It was precisely a people who had been silenced by Rome and who had lived lives of suffering despair who, seeing him come round the brow of the Mount of Olives, burst into shouting and singing: "Hosanna! Blessed is he who comes in the name of the Lord!" It all happened, just as Isaiah said it would, just as Jesus said it would, and as *Messiah* presents the text, so accurately depicting the unfolding of history.

D O you think it all Old Testament prophecy, all wonderful music, all faithful and radiantly loyal of Jesus . . . and all over? Is it all for you a fact way back there, beautiful to contemplate, but no more to be seen among us, never to be experienced in the lame and blind ways of our days? Shame upon that Christian who thus makes Christ "a dead fact, stranded on the shore." Lift up your eyes and behold him who came at Advent, and who comes.

Christ comes again in the life of a missionary's wife in Africa, who, without formal medical training, mastered the cataract operation and has restored sight to thousands, in Jesus' name. In the jungle we heard a choir of singers whose parents had heard only the beat of drums. Now they were rehearsing the Hallelujah Chorus, their ears for that mighty music being unstopped. In an Oriental clinic where the lame receive new limbs for walking, Christ is worshiped before surgery. From the rising of the sun to its going down, multitudes once dumb to the knowledge of the Lord now daily sing his praise. This, too, is history.

This Advent season, see those blind now seeing, and hear those dumb now singing. Let your heart leap up with those who walk now, and who leap for the joy in their hearts.

Amid all the rejoicings of the season, rejoice greatly in Christ. "Behold, thy King cometh unto thee." To any area of the human heart still holding out as a heathen fortress, still he comes, and he says: "You also are mine."

He is the righteous Saviour, and he shall speak peace unto your soul. Shouting and rejoicing are in order. If we were to keep silent at his coming, "the very stones would cry out."

11

AIR [CONTRALTO]

He shall feed his flock like a shepherd; and he shall gather the lambs with his arm, and carry them in his bosom, and gently lead those that are with young.

AIR [SOPRANO]

Come unto him, all ye that labour and are heavy laden, and he will give you rest. Take his yoke upon you, and learn of him, for he is meek and lowly of heart, and ye shall find rest unto your souls.

CHORUS

His yoke is easy and his burden is light.

HE who came at Advent knew the Scriptures. This *Messiah* text was familiar to him, beginning with boyhood days in Nazareth. Grown to manhood, and entering upon his ministry, Jesus said: "Come unto me, all ye that are weary and heavy laden, and I will give you rest. Take my yoke upon you, and learn of me; for I am meek and lowly in heart; and you shall find rest unto your soul." Isaiah said it first, then Jesus quoted the passage, and fulfilled it. When you hear the soprano sing the solo, let your heart be certain that it is really Christ saying to your soul: "Come unto me . . . and I will give you rest."

The invitation is as wide as the world's need, and yours. If you are heavy-laden with fear of the future, his invitation is for you. If some unconfessed and thus unforgiven sin still haunts your nights, his rest is offered to you. If you are anxious for a loved one, cast all your care on him. "I will give you rest." That is the promise which has ever been kept, and he will not fail you either. Not your faithfulness, but his, this is to be the bedrock of your confidence.

The rest which Christ gives will refresh you, and nerve your soul to go on. An unbeliever once said to E. Stanley Jones: "You believe in God, for then you have someone to hold your hand." "No," replied Jones, "I believe in God because he strengthens my arm."

A distinguished science professor had forty-seven of his students go on for their Ph.D.'s in his field. With this full scholarly life behind him, and sustained by Christian faith to which he had always held, he lay in the hospital, looking toward the campus. Just before the end, he took the president's hand and said:

> "As the marsh-hen secretly builds on the watery sod,
> Behold I will build me a nest on the greatness of God."

If, for you, life is running toward evening and you have not heard the voice of Christ for a long time, perhaps these lines describe your condition:

> "One thing strikes my heart with terror, Thy voice, O Jesus, feebler grows."

But this is Advent. Once again he comes. Once again he extends the invitation to you.

You may have been hearing him but feebly, if at all. Harden not your heart against the best you will ever know.

Augustine, that combination of brilliant mind and vagrant impulses, moved all the way from philosophy to evangelical Christianity. Writing of his pilgrimage from man's best thought to Christian faith, he said that in all the scholarly life of Greece and Rome he found no such invitation as this: "Come unto me, and I will give you rest." Let us worship God with our minds, knowing that no scholarship can yield that succor to the soul.

Perhaps the poet says it best:

"And I smiled to think God's greatness,
Flows around our incompleteness,
Round our restlessness, His rest."

COME unto me, and I will give you rest. Do not betray your soul's good by saying life is too bitter for such beauty, or that the promise is divorced from reality. Consider the New Testament setting. Immediately before Jesus said this, John had been thrown into prison. Immediately after Jesus said this, his opponents took counsel to put him to death. These words were spoken between John's prison and Christ's cross, two bitter realities. Right in the midst of the madness which beheaded John, and his own first steps toward the gallows against the sky, there Jesus said: "Come unto me, and I will give you rest." Whatever imprisons your spirits, or crucifies your best hopes, Christ says to you: "Come unto me, and I will give you rest."

With his strong hands, rough with tools and lumber, Jesus made ox yokes in the shop in Nazareth. "Take my yoke upon you," he still says. Surely it means we are to get our shoulders under the burdens of the world, and lift. But there is something even deeper here. He is quite eager to be yoked with you in whatever it is that wearies your heart.

> "O blessed burden that makes all
>   burdens light!
> O blessed yoke, that bears the bearer
>   up."

Like streams in the desert, like a cool pillow to a fevered patient, so comes this gracious invitation: "Come unto me, all ye that are weary and heavy laden, and I will give you rest." It is Christ's wondrous promise to renew the soul. Now, in Advent, reply to his invitation. In the words of the old hymn, turn to Christ and simply say:

> "O Love that will not let me go,
> I rest my weary soul in thee."

12

CHORUS

Behold the Lamb of God, that taketh away the sin of the world.

AIR [CONTRALTO]

He was despised and rejected of men; a man of sorrows and acquainted with grief.

RELIGION is man taking steps to get right with God. Christianity is God taking steps to make you right with him. Most world religions have this in common; we are not what we should be in the sight of God, and Christian faith agrees. Most faiths hold that we must take the initiative to restore the relationship. Our faith is that God took the initiative. "While we were yet sinners, Christ died for us."

Religion demands that we make amends, and make sufficient sacrifice. Christian faith holds that the sacrifice has been made: "Behold the Lamb of God, that taketh away the sin of the world." The difference is crucial, and liberating. What we could never do by ourselves is be good enough to win God's favor. Christian faith bids us to stand back and see what God has done to restore us to himself. "Behold the Lamb of God, that taketh away the sin of the world."

This difference between religion and Christianity can be seen both in primitive cultures and in highly civilized places. Years ago a man went out to rural India. In a village by a riverside he saw a mother throw her baby into the murky waters, so that both she and the child would be right with the gods. It was a costly sacrifice. How often in Western culture has a person of wealth built a temple of worship for the same reason as the village mother, both being pagans.

God has done for us what we could never do for ourselves. Whoever grasps that big idea has the beginning of sound Christian theology. Whoever allows himself to be grasped by a gracious God knows the power of being saved by grace, and not by his own goodness.

> "Nothing in my hand I bring,
> Simply to thy cross I cling."

WHEN the chorus sings, "Behold the Lamb of God," the tone color of the music darkens and the gloom begins to gather. There were shadows all along the road after Bethlehem. First there was the flight into Egypt when Jesus' family were refugees. Later he was rejected in his hometown, and harassed in the capital city. The shadows deepened into the midnight blackness of a crucifixion.

Messiah is not going to seek a way to bypass Calvary, for the Messiah did not. The way of our salvation runs through that hill shaped like a skull, not around it. He who was born came to die. That was his mission. He did not come primarily to teach, or to preach. In the intent of God, Advent was One being born for an overwhelmingly purposeful death. In Advent we lift up our hearts that he came. But he did not come to establish a perpetual Christmas spirit before he had dealt with the root cause of all our dispiritedness. Its name is sin.

There yet lingers in our culture the slightly respectable sinful view which holds that since we are comparatively virtuous, we are good Christian folk. Christianity has come to be equated with culture, education, and respectability, especially respectability. How cheap can we make grace to appear? Bonhoeffer answers:

"Cheap grace is the preaching of forgiveness without requiring repentance, baptism without church discipline, Communion without confession, absolution without contrition. Cheap grace is grace without discipleship, grace without the cross, grace without Jesus Christ, living and incarnate. . . . Costly grace is the gospel which must be *sought* again and again, the gift which must be *asked* for, the door at which a man must *knock*."

THE first snowfall of the year usually comes during Advent. The sparkling beauty of a winter morning can be dazzling. When that first white blanket is drawn over nature it is beautiful, for it covers harsh reality. All the scars we have made in nature disappear, at least for the moment. All the trash heaps and all the garbage dumps of the world are mercifully covered from sight. The heart should cry, "Can those within be covered, also?" We should be thankful for a brief relief from the daily view. But to stop with that view is cheap grace. Look on the new beauty in nature, and know in your heart the truth of the Scripture: "Though your sins be as scarlet, they shall be as white as snow."

If we look only at the beauty of nature during Advent, we may miss the meeting with nature's God. If, amid the good cheer of the season, we say only that God is love, we may miss the crucial nature of love, which is to suffer. William Temple wrote: "To say that God is love may carry us but a little way if we have not Christ upon the cross before our mind; it may even be misleading."

In Advent, *Messiah* leads us to the deepest understanding of the love of God. He does come. It is the gracious bending down of God to our human condition. He does speak in tenderest terms to our weary hearts. We have heard those kindest of words. But he did not come primarily with words, or even works. He came to die.

Advent began in the heart of God. He who came forth from the Father returned there. But not until he did for us what we could never do for ourselves. "Behold the Lamb of God, that taketh away the sin of the world." O come, let us adore him.

13

AIR [CONTRALTO]

Surely he hath borne our griefs, and carried our sorrows. He was wounded for our transgressions; he was bruised for our iniquities; the chastisement of our peace was upon him.

CHORUS

And with his stripes we are healed.

CHORUS

All we like sheep have gone astray; we have turned every one to his own way. And the Lord hath laid on him the iniquity of us all.

SACRIFICE for others is the human condition of goodness. Only the hopelessly self-centered will fail to see it. At our birth there was pain, and who knows the long night vigils of mother that we might have rest. Some teacher's faithfulness inspired us most, even if we knew it not until years later, and perhaps the teacher never did know. The surgeon's long and lonely hours of preparation were the sacrifice that his scalpel may excise our deep hurt. A father works and saves, and amid weary years goes right on working and saving, in order that his son or daughter may get a better education than he had. A college president would say to the freshmen in the presence of their parents at the opening convocation: "Your parents would rather see you receive a degree than view the Taj Mahal by moonlight."

If the human condition is made sweeter by sacrifice, how much more our relationship to God. "He was wounded for our transgressions." There stands our eternal deserving of nothing at all, and the sacrifice of Christ which fills our hands and our hearts with the best that life can hold. "With his stripes we are healed."

In the back country there is a saying: "If you see a turtle on a stump, you can be sure he didn't get there by himself." There is humor and deep truth. Look back over your own life. The tender care of earliest years, the barest needs of food and dress, the best ideals you know, and the most cherished memories—most were the result of someone else's doing, often in humble and almost unknown ways. We are all bound in the bundle of life, and the cord of pure gold which holds each self together bears one shining truth—"I am what the sacrifice of others has done for me."

I watched her in the loud and shadowy lanes
Of life; and every face that passed her by
Grew calmly restful, smiling quietly,
As though she gave for all their griefs and pains
Largesse of comfort, soft as summer rains
And balsam tinctured with tranquillity.
Yet in her own eyes dwelt an agony.
"Oh, halcyon soul," I cried, "what sorrow reigns
In that calm heart, which knows such ways to heal?"
She said—"Where balms are made for human uses,
Great furnace fires, and wheel on grinding wheel
Must crush and purify the crude herb juices;
And in some hearts the conflict cannot cease:
They are the sick world's factories of peace."

"The chastisement of our peace was upon

him." It is the law of life, caught up into the purposes of God, the lawgiver and the redeemer. You can be at peace with yourself, but not because you deserve peace, for you know better than that, but because he is your peace. In Jesus Christ, God accepts you, even though in the depths you consider yourself unacceptable. This self-acceptance you now have is health, because you are dealing with yourself as you are, perhaps for the first time. The fantasy self, which seeks so many ways for acceptance, is no longer necessary. Pride and self-striving are gone. The authentic self stands forth. You were loved all the way to the cross. There the chastisement of your peace was upon him. And with his stripes you were healed.

IT is the naked realism of Christian faith that elicits our response. God does not insult us by saying our sins don't really matter. We know differently, and so does he. Transgressions and iniquities are accurate descriptions. May we be too honest to give them any other names. A God who forgives without suffering would be an insult, not a saviour. He was wounded for our transgressions.

"If we have never sought, we seek Thee now;
　Thine eyes burn through the dark, our only stars;
We must have sight of thorn-pricks on Thy brow,
　We must have Thee, O Jesus of the scars.

"The heavens frighten us; they are too calm;
　In all the universe we have no place.
Our wounds are hurting us. Where is the balm?

O Jesus, by Thy scars we claim Thy
   grace."

Before his mother saw his face in Bethlehem, she had that dark foreboding: "In
you shall all the nations of the world be
blessed . . . and a sword shall pierce your
heart." How often deepest joy and deepest
sorrow lie close together.

It is right that we should rejoice as we,
with Mary, await the day of his birth. There
is an even deeper joy at the center of the soul.
It is in the simple knowledge that "he was
wounded for our transgressions; he was
bruised for our iniquities; the chastisement
of our peace was upon him; . . . and with his
stripes we are healed." Surely this is "love
divine, all loves excelling." And we are
known, and held, and will be kept by his
suffering love forever.

14

RECITATIVE [TENOR]   ACCOMPANIED

All they that see him, laugh him to scorn; they shoot out their lips, and shake their heads, saying:

CHORUS

He trusted in God that he would deliver him; let him deliver him, if he delight in him.

RECITATIVE [TENOR]   ACCOMPANIED

Thy rebuke hath broken his heart; he is full of heaviness. He looked for someone to have pity on him, but there was no man; neither found he any to comfort him.

NEITHER found he any to comfort him. *Messiah* opens with that powerful word to our souls: "Comfort ye, comfort ye my people." Our minds are bade to reflect on the comfort which God is preparing for us in the coming of one at Advent. But this long dark passage which we have been contemplating closes with these words: "Neither found he any to comfort him." We are simply to reflect on the desolation and the inner anguish. He who was all comfort to so many, and whose coming was announced with the first and best word, "Comfort ye," is the very one who finds no one to comfort him. At the end he is alone. We really should say, "My God, my God, why have we forsaken thee?"

Humanly speaking, "Neither found he any to comfort him." Yet in the depths of it all he could say, "Father, into thy hands I commit my spirit." Whoever can say "Father" in the midst of the worst is neither alone nor without comfort. Jesus gave us that name for God.

Do you live with the daily conviction that God is indeed worthy of the name Father? We mean by the name that God is the perfect union of power and love. Nothing can separate us from that power and that love, except our own sin. Hold your hand between your eyes and the sun, and light is dimmed. Keep a desert between your eyes and the sun, and light is dimmed. Keep a desert between yourself and the river, and no stream sings at your feet. Live as though God were not, and neither his power nor his love will be known.

There is a Godforsakenness of the soul, but it is not that God has abandoned us. We may simply have lived as though he were not. But just when the desolation seems total, and the aloneness complete, right there you may say: "I found him nearest when I missed him most." Father, into thy hands.

PERHAPS the cruelest mockery in which the human heart ever engaged is here described. "He trusted in God . . .; let him deliver him if he delight in him." He who most trusted in God is accused of having no trust. Who can measure that rebuke? Would it not break any heart? To do his Father's will was all his desire, and to be obedient even unto death was the measure of his commitment and his trust. When he prayed that his will would not be done, but that his Father's will should be accomplished, he was committing himself for life or death.

The shallowness of his critics is revealed in their simplistic view of religion. If God really delighted in him, then deliverance from the cross would surely be granted. It is a view still fighting for acceptance within us when life is rough and tragedy threatens. Sometimes it is openly expressed: "Trust God, he will heal . . . he will solve . . . he will deliver." If the most obedient and most trusting person the world has ever seen was not delivered, who among us can claim exemption?

The superficial soul leaps to the conclusion that if God does not deliver, it is a sign he does not love. How totally unbiblical is that position. Egypt's lash was felt for forty years without deliverance. Yet God was nation-building, forging his children into a people in Egypt. Babylon's captivity was sorely borne by Israel: "We hanged our harps on the willow tree, yea, we wept when we remembered Zion." Isaiah foresaw the coming of Messiah, where? It was in the midnight darkness of Babylon.

Do all you can to relieve suffering, and praise God for the skill that heals. But when there is no relief or healing, what then? Then you are suffering as Christ suffered, without deliverance. Father, into thy hands.

S O we have worked through the last of the long *Messiah* passages dealing with the death of the Messiah. Have we been restless under the discipline of the protracted darkness? A person who will not face Christ's death honestly will scarcely face his own life courageously. Our facile confidence about the future and our too chirpy optimism about human nature have now been exposed. Chastened by the bitterness of things, we may cry out against a world we did not make, and would not choose.

Thank God the record of his life did not end with the crowds shouting, "Blessed is he that cometh in the name of the Lord." If it had ended there, the bitterness of things which we have known would have ended our interest in him.

The weight of the Old Testament is that life is grim, with some goodness, under God. The weight of the New Testament is that God is good, and he is suffering love. We see it clearly, not in the blossoming fields but in

111

Gethsemane, not in the crowds that followed him but in the cross where he was nailed. "Neither found he any to comfort him."

For the Biblical description of things as they are, for the New Testament clarity about suffering love, for One who came in a woman's pain, and went from loss of blood and exposure, thanks be to thee, O God, praise be to thee, O Christ.

"Reality, reality,
Lord Jesus Christ, thou art to me."

Father, into thy hands.

15

AIR [TENOR]

Behold, and see if there be any sorrow like unto his sorrow.

RECITATIVE [TENOR]   ACCOMPANIED

He was cut off out of the land of the living; for the transgression of thy people was he stricken.

AIR [TENOR]

But thou didst not leave his soul in hell; nor didst thou suffer thy Holy One to see corruption.

ANEW star shone in the skies the night Christ came. Darkness hung over the hill the day he went. Between his coming and his going we have walked in Galilee, listened to the rippling of the Jordan, heard his gracious words, and watched a multitude acclaim him with palm branches and shouts of joy. But we have also seen the lonely road from his hometown to the capital, heard him slandered and witnessed his whipping, seen his closest friends slip away from the action into the shadows, and heard the dull thud of the hammer as the nails were driven through the flesh into the wood. "Friend, it is over now, the passion, the sweat, the pains, only the truth remains."

Right here we must searchingly ask, What truth remains? Some have said the truth of his example remains. Yes, it does, but how does that help? He was sinless, can you match that example? He prayed without ceasing, do we? He continued to love when his whole world turned loveless, could we?

115

No, as an example he is simply outsized for us. Thank God he did not say: "Imitate me." That would have convicted us of a daily disobedience.

Some have said that what remains is the truth of his teaching. True, in part, yet consider these things. He said he was the light of the world, but that light flickered out on Calvary. He said he was the good shepherd, but that shepherd died and the sheep scattered. Again he said: "He who believes in me shall never die," but he who made that claim simply died himself. Poor bankrupt faith that is centered in his teaching, for if when he died, he died forever, then much of the teaching is fraud, and his claims are the claims of an impostor. This must be faced, and grasped in the depths of our being.

WITH what quiet restraint *Messiah* lays before us the central fact of history, and of faith. "But thou didst not leave his soul in hell; nor didst thou suffer thy Holy One to see corruption." With one lightning flash, struck from the midnight of Christ's death, God illumines the universe.

The resurrection of Jesus Christ is the rock on which we stand. At this point all philosophies and all religions pale. God is the supreme director of this cosmic drama. Advent began in the mind of God, for it was his purpose to act redemptively. That redemption was not accomplished by the teaching or by the example of Jesus Christ. No, it was through his devotion unto death, and the mighty act of God, who "brought again from the dead our Lord Jesus Christ." Miss this, and you miss it all. "Only the truth remains."

The death of Christ is the best reason in the world for being an atheist. He was the finest person who ever lived. He was the teacher *par excellence*. He was humble, honest, courageous, and radiantly loyal to his ideals. If that man who died on the cross at the hands of religious people is dead forever, then either God does not exist or we should despise him.

Do not base your unbelief on the indifference of nature, or the tragedies of history, or your own suffering. Nature can be nurturing, history has some high drama of human goodness, and suffering can be borne, even transmuted. Take higher ground for your unbelief. Center it on the death of history's noblest soul. At age thirty-three he was crucified, dead, and buried. There is the most solid base for outright atheism, or that lurking area of unbelief back there in the dark corner of life.

IT is either that black despair or a historical fact to which *Messiah* points: "But thou didst not leave his soul in hell; nor didst thou suffer thy Holy One to see corruption." That event, the resurrection of Jesus Christ, established the church, wrote the New Testament, and sent Christianity flaming through the ancient world. Neither our own faith nor the witness of the church can ultimately rest on any foundation other than the chief cornerstone, the resurrection.

When you stand on your own personal Calvary and endure some crucifixion of the good, or when history's wreckage keeps you from seeing any pattern or purpose, remember:

"Judge not the Play before the Play is
   done;
Her Plot has many changes; every day
Speaks a new scene; the last act crowns
   the Play."

First act—Advent, and the coming of

One to fulfill the heart's deep longing. Second act—that life incomparable. Third act—the top of a lonely hill, and shuddering death. But: "Judge not the Play before the Play is done; . . . the last act crowns the Play!"

In the last act the Director of the drama "did not leave his soul in hell." The resurrection of Christ is truth, cosmic and eternal truth. His teaching concerning himself was validated by the resurrection. It is the victory of God over the evil, and the wickedness and the stupidity of humanity. It is the heart of our assurance. This is the victory—the rock of our confidence. God is in charge of the universe.

The destiny of the world process, the last act, will be in the hands of God. He who initiated the cosmic process will draw the final curtain. The last act will be under the personal direction of the Author.

16

Lift up your heads, O ye gates; and be ye lifted up, ye everlasting doors; and the King of glory shall come in. Who is the King of glory? The Lord strong and mighty, the Lord mighty in battle. The Lord of Hosts, he is the King of glory.

THE gates were the most important part of an ancient city. They were the only means of access through the high and fortified wall. By day there passed through the gates all the colorful pageant of life. Camel caravans, peasants on donkeys, soldiers on foot and on horseback, and the ordinary folk who had gone out to work in the fields, all entered the city through the gates, and before sundown. At night the gates were closed, and strengthened with bars of brass or iron.

What shall we say of those areas of our hearts, barred with stronger bars than any of brass or iron? We have forged barriers against the entrance of the things of the spirit. We have subtle strategies of the self to keep Christ outside the walls of the real person. If the Lord of Hosts were to come with an army, we could flee. If he were to come into our darkness simply as a man with a searchlight, we could hide. But when he comes in Advent as a little child, whose heart is hard enough to resist? Our hearts are hard enough, they really are. For the news of Advent is just too good.

When Cornwallis surrendered at Yorktown, a messenger carrying the news set out for the then distant Philadelphia. He crossed the river by ferry, changed horses several times, and arrived in the city nearly exhausted from the long ordeal. In the early morning hours he hammered at the door of the president of the Continental Congress. A zealous night watchman threatened to arrest him for disturbing the peace. His news was just too good.

It is so with this Advent claim that the Lord of Hosts, he who is almighty, is all meekness too. We are accustomed to the swagger of power and the innocence of weakness. The world and our hearts cry out for one who is at once almighty, and all loving. In Christ there is no conflict between his meekness and his might. He identified with the fallen, and little children trusted him, yet he drove the money changers from the Temple in holy wrath. His meekness is coupled with his might, and that is precisely why he is the most attractive and winsome figure in all history.

LIFT up your heads, O ye gates. The gate is an important Biblical figure. In the Old Testament the word "gate" is sometimes used to mean power or dominion. God promises Abraham that his posterity shall have a better world: "Your descendants shall possess the gate of their enemies." Entrenched evil, power without compassion, wickedness in seats of authority—you can readily name the enemies you want your posterity to possess.

Again, if there is still some area of your own life holding out against the entrance of Christ and the middle years are hurrying by, take courage from that passage in Ezekiel: "The gate shall not be shut until evening."

When the church seems something less than an army with banners, going forth with spiritual power, then come over into the New Testament and hear the strong assurance of Christ: "I will build my church; and the gates of hell shall not prevail against it." Christ alone is the rock of our confidence concerning the church.

There are Christians who have an exclusive view of their relationship to God, as though their way were the only way into the divine presence at the end of history. But in the book of Revelation there is the forthright statement that there are twelve gates to the city of God.

Consider the wondrous imagery of that last book of the Bible, a poetic pointing to eternal reality: "The city has no need of sun or moon to shine upon it, for the glory of God is its light, and its lamp is the Lamb. By its light shall the nations walk; and the kings of the earth shall bring their glory into it, and its gates shall never be shut by day—and there shall be no night there." What a telling way to show that the gates of God's mercy are ever open. The gates are never closed while it is day, and there is no night!

WHO is the King of glory? *Messiah* reiterates this passage again and again. Hear the full chorus, asking over and over, "Who is the King of glory?" The repetition is for good cause. Unless we know the answer to that question, we will never know peace. Advent provides the answer.

In the same Twenty-fourth Psalm from which *Messiah* takes this whole passage, there are also the familiar lines:

"Who shall ascend into the hill of the
    Lord?
Or who shall stand in his holy place?
He that hath clean hands, and a pure
    heart;
Who hath not lifted up his soul unto
    vanity,
Nor sworn deceitfully."

For now, through him, his life and death, and rising again, we have clean hands, and by his grace alone is the heart purified.

Despite all our wanderings of mind and dullness of spirit, despite all our foolishness which has not worn out God's patience, despite the stinging sin and the hard self, there stands the invitation and the promise: "Lift up your heads, O ye gates; and be ye lifted up, ye everlasting doors; and the King of glory shall come in."

There is an old Advent hymn, based on this very passage of *Messiah*. May we hear it in the heart's deep core.

"Lift up your heads, ye mighty gates,
Behold, the King of glory waits;
The King of kings is drawing near;
The Saviour of the world is here!"

We are to answer that invitation. It is our soul's health in Advent, simply to say in the words of the third stanza:

"Redeemer, come! I open wide
My heart to Thee; here, Lord, abide.
Let me Thy inner presence feel;
Thy grace and love in me reveal." Amen.

17

AIR [SOPRANO]

How beautiful are the feet of them that preach the gospel of peace, and bring glad tidings of good things.

CHORUS

Their sound is gone out into all lands, and their words unto the ends of the world.

CHRISTMAS is the season for others. At least once a year the whole atmosphere is charged with concern that no one will have a cheerless day. Complete strangers wish each other the season's best. Somehow that reticence and reserve which marks our usual manner is broken through by a spirit not our own, and we find ourselves extending greetings and warm best wishes to almost casual acquaintances. We find ourselves asking, Why cannot life be like this always?

We are deeply to understand that this feeling we have toward others at Christmas is a miniature of the feeling of God toward all the world. The "glad tidings of good things" is the daily message we are to share, year in and year out, with the whole human family, everywhere. "Their sound is gone out into all lands, and their words unto the ends of the world." Isaiah said it first, under inspiration. Christ commanded it. Our distinction is that we are to share the high endeavor of those who preach the gospel of peace to every land under heaven.

Bishop Azariah of India, over a period of twenty-five years, received a quarter of a million outcasts into Christian faith. "I used to have them place their hands on their heads as if in the act of baptism, and repeat after me: 'I am a baptized Christian. Woe is me if I preach not the gospel.'" Here in our passage, *Messiah* is heralding the gospel of peace.

What has it all amounted to, this world mission of Christ? Simply this: amid all the fracturing of our common humanity, and despite the powerful differences among the nations, there is a community of Christ's people on which the sun never sets. The gospel has gone out into all lands. That is solid historical fact. And if there are divisions and strivings among the peoples of the world, there is also a healing and reconciling fellowship that leaps over all boundaries and binds humanity with chains of gold to the throne of God. That, too, is reality.

ROUNDING the bend of a jungle road in Africa, little more than a trail through the forest, a group came upon a cemetery. Here lay all that was mortal of physicians, teachers, and evangelists, who had left all for that more excellent call to follow Christ without reservation. A few years earlier the United States ambassador to the United Nations had traveled in that region. This is what he wrote: "Anyone who travels there is constantly reminded of their heroism. Missionaries laid a groundwork in religion, health, and education under difficult and dangerous circumstances. What they have done is almost beyond belief. They fought yellow fever, dysentery, parasites. And the gravestones I saw! My God, their gravestones—all through Africa."

What is true of that land is true of all six continents. They were your fellow Christians. They are your fellow Christians still. Only now they look steadily at the Light which never fades, in the communion of saints.

Are we following their work with our lives, our prayers, and our money? Alfred North Whitehead was no evangelist, but he knew the heart of the matter. "Above and beyond all things, the religious life is not a research after comfort. . . . The worship of God is not a rule of safety—it is an adventure of the spirit, a flight after the unattainable. The death of religion comes with the repression of the high hope of adventure."

To receive Christ at Advent is to go with him in spirit to the ends of the earth. A narrower view is selfish, not Scriptural. He who came is he who said, "Go ye." To accept his coming without offering to share his going is an act of pure self-centeredness. Of course we go in many ways. Our money and our prayers are minimal marks of discipleship. The saddest obituary you could have would be: "The world mission of Christ received no help from me."

THEIR sound is gone out into all lands, and their words unto the ends of the world. This is the season when we turn to familiar literature and the hope is that the best of it will seize us afresh. Henry van Dyke puts these words into the mouth of old Abgarus when "the other wise man" was starting on his travels: "I am too old for this journey, but my heart shall be a companion of the pilgrimage day and night, and I shall know the end of thy quest." The end of the quest is that Bethlehem of the heart's desire, where we shall know as we have been known, and where we shall understand, as all along we have been understood by the God of Bethlehem.

"Glad tidings of good things." When the soprano sings it in *Messiah* we know it is deeply true. And thus Scripture brings us full circuit, from the going out into all lands back to our soul's need. The glad tidings which have been going forth to the ends of the earth for centuries come afresh at this season. He who has been going is he who eternally comes. Advent is the glad tidings of God for a weary world, and to each heart that will prepare him room. May it be so with our souls.

"O Zion, haste, thy mission high
     fulfilling,
   To tell to all the world that God is
   Light,
That he who made all nations is not
   willing
   One soul should perish, lost in shades
   of night.
Publish glad tidings, tidings of peace,
Tidings of Jesus, redemption and
   release."

18

AIR [BASS]

Why do the nations so furiously rage together, and why do the people imagine a vain thing? The kings of the earth rise up, and the rulers take counsel together against the Lord, and against his Anointed.

CHORUS

Let us break their bonds asunder, and cast away their yokes from us.

RECITATIVE [TENOR]

He that dwelleth in heaven shall laugh them to scorn; the Lord shall have them in derision.

AIR [TENOR]

Thou shalt break them with a rod of iron; thou shalt dash them in pieces like a potter's vessel.

THOU shalt break them with a rod of iron; Thou shalt dash them in pieces like a potter's vessel. We begin with that knotty closing passage. However we interpret these words, it is clear that the psalmist is reserving to God alone sovereignty over history. Lose sight of that and we lose all.

Grim and savage language, it was appropriate in its day. We may soften the vocabulary; we dare not take away the consequences of rebellion against the rule of God. Not many would claim that God so directly intervenes in the affairs of nations. But to believe that humanity can do as it pleases with impunity is to fly in the face of both history and Scripture. We have a more Christlike view of God than the old Hebrew, but to explain away all passages referring to judgment is to explain away the action of God in history. The fact of judgment is a perennial aspect of life under God. It is the nature and purpose of that divine judgment which is more clearly understood since Christ came.

"Between the wrath of God and most of what this world calls wrath, no parallel exists. Between them there is no connection, no faintest resemblance at all. . . . The wrath of God is the totality of the divine reaction to sin. Everything that man's rebellion against the moral order brings upon him—suffering for his body, hardening of his heart, blinding for his faculty of inward vision—is included in that reaction. Is this punishment? Yes, certainly; but it is not God's outraged dignity retaliating by a direct penal act. Rather it is the sinner who punishes himself."

Immediately preceding this judgment passage the psalmist writes: "You are my son, today I have begotten you. Ask of me, and I will make the nations your heritage, and the ends of the earth your possession." We can trust the divine judgment that brings the nations and the ends of the earth to Christ.

WHY do the nations so furiously rage together . . .? The kings of the earth rise up, and the rulers take counsel together. Clearly this is a conspiracy to overthrow authority. Their aim is to free themselves from a ruler. Whenever a sovereign died, or there was a new accession to power, rebellions would brew. How was it to be accomplished? "Let us break their bonds asunder, and cast away their yokes from us."

Here is a parallel of humanity's perennial rebellion against the good. Discipline is in order to freedom, but who wants to pay that price? When a leading university confers law degrees, the dean always refers to "those wise restraints which make men free."

If we rebel against the good, how much more against God? "Break bonds asunder . . . cast away yokes"—how often such language would describe the human spirit against the spirit of the living God.

"She set a rose to blossom in her hair,

The day faith died;
'Now glad,' she said, 'and free I go,
   And life is wide' . . .
But through long nights she stared into
   the dark,
   And knew she lied."

There is a familiar caricature that gathers up the modern view of the divine absence. "Darwin banished God from life. Newton banished God from the universe. Freud banished God from the soul."

In this passage of *Messiah* go back now and read those not-so-strange words: "He that dwelleth in heaven shall laugh." On Biblical authority we may attribute a sense of humor to deity. How else could human foibles be tolerated in heaven?

THE original psalm was written on the occasion of a king's succession to the throne as an expression of confidence in his power to rule. The entire passage can be read simply as a tribute to the one in authority, in spite of all opposition. Seeing it in that light, with what confidence the Christian views Christ's kingship. "Men may have to wait long for the enthronement of Christ over the world as seen from the earth; but it is already a fact in God's purpose. In the realm of the real there is no other King but Jesus."

Most of this passage from *Messiah* is quoted verbatim in the book of Acts, when the disciples were gathered together following the crucifixion and resurrection. "The Gentiles rage. . . . The kings of the earth set themselves in array . . . against the Lord and against his Anointed." Then, to recall that enmity toward Christ which they have just witnessed, they say this in striking parallel: "Truly in this city there were gathered together against thy holy servant Jesus, whom thou didst anoint, both Herod and Pontius pilate, with the Gentiles and the peoples of Israel, to do whatever thy hand and thy plan had predestined to take place." It was humanity's grossest folly, but God used that evil for our greatest good. Here is a view of history that looks open-eyed at the worst, and knows the living God is still sovereign.

Modern testimony comes very movingly from a Nazi concentration camp. From prison Martin Niemoeller wrote: "I am firmly convinced that all attempts in the way of the holy gospel must serve the sole purpose of increasing its impelling force. . . . I see this so clearly in my own case. . . . I believe my incarceration is an instance of God's holy sense of humor. Here they laugh scornfully 'at last we have got him,' and arrest eight hundred more, but what is the result? Full churches with praying congregations. It would be utter ingratitude to become bitter in the face of such facts."

God's laughter seems strange language, but it is essential to see that faith uses humor for its purposes. The purpose of history is redemptive. Hence we can smile, amid our tears, for God is sovereign in history, and over all.

19

Hallelujah! For the Lord God omnipotent reigneth. The kingdom of this world is become the kingdom of our Lord, and of his Christ; and he shall reign for ever and ever.

King of Kings, and Lord of Lords. Hallelujah!

WORDS are quite inadequate to describe a sunset over Galilee, the wonder in a child's face, or the beauty of Mont Blanc when the sun bursts through to illumine the already dazzling whiteness with a light ineffable. How much more difficult to say anything at all after we have stood for the Hallelujah Chorus. Multitudes have found here the peak point of the oratorio. What the Magna Charta is for constitution-writing, and what Shakespeare is for casting the whole of life in dramatic form, so this chorus would be named by an innumerable host as that high juncture of music and faith, producing the hallowed assurance of the divine.

Through an everlasting mercy the trumpets do sound in the soul. The goodness and the kindness and the love which once we knew arouse as if from long sleep. Our finest nature comes forward, and we behold the true self like a long-lost friend. If not seized and cherished, the moment passes, and the soul returns to sleep again, to a long sleep.

Your spiritual chance is in that finest moment. Lengthen it, nourish it, say to that nobility within you: "This is the person I can become." For if you don't, life will lull you to sleep again, smother you in convention again, choke you with success again, choke you to death, spiritually.

The burning desire to have that buried self be more and more your true self is the finest gift we can bring to Christ at Christmas. Let *Messiah* do its good work in the soul's deep places, then rise in faith to that height you know as fact when the chorus calls you to worship him who is "King of Kings, and Lord of Lords." Move in sincere intent toward:

> "The high that proved too high, the
>   heroic for earth too hard,
>   The passion that left the ground to lose
>   itself in the sky,
> Are music sent up to God. . . ."

AND he shall reign. The gospel is personal, but it is also cosmic. The promise is not only that individuals are saved but also that history is to be redeemed. There is a fulfillment of history worthy of the life, and death, and rising again of our Lord Jesus Christ.

Scripture is not crystal clear as to whether this consummation is to take place within the historical process or whether it stands at the end of history. When the disciples asked Jesus about some details of the kingdom he replied: "It is not for you to know times or seasons which the Father has fixed by his own authority." Did their not knowing the specifics keep them from fulfilling their duty? Those words of Jesus are in the first chapter of Acts, and the remainder of the book is aflame with their devotion. We are not given a blueprint, we are given a promise, sealed with death and resurrection: "And he shall reign."

Meanwhile the ambiguities of history and the power of evil always stand menacing the

149

human spirit, threatening to drive out saving faith:

> "Things fall apart; the center cannot
>   hold;
> Mere anarchy is loosed upon the
>   world. . . .
> The best lack all conviction, while the
>   worst
> Are full of passionate intensity."

Ambiguity and bafflement are destined to be with us, perhaps until the end of time. But whether in our time or at the end of time, God shall reign. No contrived climax on this planet will take God by surprise. Man cannot usurp God's power. He can share it, using or misusing the power God places in his hands. But man cannot usurp God's power and eclipse his Maker. He may eclipse himself. But final power and the final destiny of the universe is in God. He has not given that final destiny into any other hands. He shall reign, and he reigns now.

WE go back to the personal. The first public performance of *Messiah* was on April 13, 1742, in Dublin. Ladies were requested not to wear hoops, and gentlemen were asked not to wear their swords. Neither high style nor raw power was to have any standing before the Prince of Peace who comes at Advent. If we could put away our pride, and all the protective armor we wear over our real selves, we would know in our own hearts: "He shall reign for ever and ever." For the word of God became flesh, and is very personal. It is for you.

"He shall reign for ever." "This is clearly the promise, speaking to our human hopes from beyond. The divine promise is so clearly not an extension of human hope alone. The human heart is unable as it is to truly will the kingdom of God in its sinful nature. So—Jeremiah says He will write his law upon our hearts. This fulfillment, yet from beyond, is the meaning of the promise of the reign forever and ever—witnessing to the fact that He is Lord."

Someone ventured clumsily into Handel's room when he had just written the last notes of the Hallelujah Chorus. The great work lay finished before him. With tears streaming down his face, Handel exclaimed, "I did think I did see all heaven before me, and the great God himself."

May it be so with *Messiah* lovers for ages to come, for the purpose of it all is that we may see God, which is the promise to those whose hearts have been purified by his coming. Let our highest praise be given, not to Handel, or to any music, but to the Lord God omnipotent. He it is who shall reign forever and ever. Amen.

20

I know that my Redeemer liveth, and that he shall stand at the latter day upon the earth; and though worms destroy this body, yet in my flesh shall I see God.

For now is Christ risen from the dead, the first fruits of them that sleep.

I KNOW that my Redeemer liveth. Beauty and truth are wedded in this text. The soprano solo has sung its way into saddened lives at their darkest moment, and has been used by God to transform the shadows into light and glory. It is a high and hauntingly lovely refrain, dealing with the low and harsh fact of the decomposition of the body, and, grasping that truth unflinchingly, faces its passingness and temporality in luminous trust: "I know that my Redeemer liveth."

The rock of Christian confidence is right there: "For now is Christ risen from the dead." We are not asked to believe that a future life is ours by right, a straining of credulity for the honest person. We are not asked to believe that immortality is our nature, in the face of that biological truth that worms destroy this body. We are called by God, and invited to trust his everlasting mercy to grant us the gift of resurrection. It will be his doing, not our nature, or our deserving.

The fact of resurrection leaps from the Gospel records, empowers The Acts of the Apostles, and informs every page that follows in the New Testament. Mary had seen Jesus in the garden. Cleopas had talked with him on the road to Emmaus. Thomas had touched his wounds. The disciples had that reunion with him in familiar haunts by the Sea of Galilee. They had all met him again in the upper room. He who had died was now their daily companion and living Lord, in a relationship that death would only make perfect.

There came a day when Sir James Simpson, discoverer of chloroform and pioneer in the science of medicine, saw his little daughter pass from this life to where, beyond all suffering, there is peace. Over her grave in the cemetery in Edinburgh is the memorial stone, bearing her name and these words: "Nevertheless I live."

FOR now is Christ risen from the dead, the first fruits of them that sleep. Here we are led right into the communion of saints. Resurrection is no solitary experience, but that uniting with all who have preceded us into the divine presence. It is a noble company—Paul, Augustine, Martin Luther, Pope John XXIII, and your own beloved dead. And it is not just such exemplars of faith, but farmers, fisherfolk, factory hands, and all who lived their undistinguished lives with quiet trust. Think also of those whose writing have illumined the human spirit:

"Call me not dead when I have gone
Into the company of the ever-living.
Let thanksgiving rather be made.
Say: 'Now, at last, he hath won release.
Today, perhaps, wandering in starry
  places,
He hath met Keats, and known him by
  his eyes.
Tomorrow, who can say, Shakespeare

157

may pass,
Or Milton, or Dante, looking on the
  grass
Thinking of Beatrice, and listening still
To triumphant hymns, far-sounding
  from the hill.'"

Every person who lives with an aching emptiness where once there was a dear face, now beheld no more, should have this quiet trust: "Some day the bell will sound, Some day my heart will bound, As with a shout, That school is out, And, lessons done, I homeward run." Home is reunion, and joy, and love.

Especially when we receive the bread and the cup we are to remember that we have come to "the spirits of just men made perfect" and that Christ is indeed "the first fruits of them that sleep." We, and they, feed on Christ, the living bread. This is the communion of saints.

AS we turn to our ordinary lives, we can live with a certain gaiety of spirit: "Whether I live or whether I die, I am the Lord's." When this resurrection faith becomes lodged in our deepest consciousness, its beneficent work enables us to carry on with courage, knowing that the best is yet to be. We are to live by the power of this resurrection faith, knowing that "death, a necessary end, will come when it will come." No one should court death, but every believer in Christ's resurrection is to be certain of his own. A twentieth-century disciple wrote: "When I die, friends, don't stall around. Cremate, or bury my bones. Have a short memorial service next Sunday afternoon to comfort my loved ones, then go on about your business. Don't mourn for me. I'll be in the Presence, whereas you will still be fighting taxes and bombs. Mourn for yourselves."

Concerning our own future, if our faith is centered in Christ, we should live in the full Biblical assurance. Handel's *Messiah*, a lyrical stating of Scripture, together with the setting of his entombment, summons us to such quiet confidence. His last resting-place is Westminster Abbey. A sculptured figure of the composer stands serenely in that hallowed place. In his hand are a few bars of music. The inscribed text is simply: "I know that my Redeemer liveth." Knowing the redeemer, you can both live and die in peace.

21

CHORUS

Since by man came death,
By man came also the resurrection of the
dead.
For as in Adam all die,
Even so in Christ shall all be made alive.

RECITATIVE [BASS]   ACCOMPANIED

Behold, I tell you a mystery: We shall not
all sleep, but we shall all be changed in a
moment, in the twinkling of an eye, at the
last trumpet.

AIR [BASS]

The trumpet shall sound, and the dead
shall be raised incorruptible, and we shall
be changed.

AWISE man said he did not fully understand the doctrine of original sin, but he clearly saw that sin was universal. The origin may be obscure, the ubiquity is obvious. To express the fact of our distance from God and our deserving of no destiny, try this shorthand: "In Adam all die." That is our human nature, and nature's destiny. Then, having seen the resurrection of Christ, and having experienced the forgiveness of sins, gather it all up: "Even so in Christ shall all be made alive."

In his natural body, like yours and mine, Jesus had been seen, known, and loved. Then he died. Then he was seen, known, and loved after his death. There was change, but there was persistence of personality, and there was identity. "The dead shall be raised incorruptible," Paul wrote. The followers had seen it so in Christ, and they knew he would do the same for them. They were not theorizing about immortality, a futile exercise. They were reporting an experience of resurrection.

Paul refers to there being a natural body, and a spiritual body. There is a natural body, which we bury in the earth. There is a spiritual body, which God gives us forever. It really is that logical. This body does not last very long. The body that God gives us is of the nature of the eternal order.

"Behold, I tell you a mystery." In a mysterious natural universe Scripture is not pretending that all truth is as clear as sunlight on the Sea of Galilee. There are depths to the lake, and to life, and to truth. But there is One who knows all depths, and all life, and all truth. There is a charming story that still makes the rounds in Princeton. Someone said to Mrs. Einstein one day, "Do you know all about relativity?" "No," she replied, "but I know my husband, and I know he can be trusted." You do not need to know all about life, and death, and eternity, if you know Jesus Christ, risen from the dead.

WE shall be changed. Thank God. That word from *Messiah* may not have grasped you before. It is very precious to a person who has seen eighty summers but whose sight is failing, and to a thirty-year-old who was struck by polio in childhood. They will be given a body that preserves identity and in which personality persists, a body in which each will be tenderly made perfect.

Diminishing powers and the eroding of vitality are our fate. Who has said it more poignantly than Ruskin, who wrote so well of art and beauty? "Oh, why did no one tell me that the colours would fade, and that the glory of the earth would vanish; and that the soul asks and must have something . . . more splendid than this earth can give." That is a cry out of the depths. He should have read what Paul wrote to that little church in Corinth: "No eye has seen, nor ear heard, nor the heart of man conceived, what God has prepared for those who love him." But Paul immediately goes on to say that those who look to the resurrected Christ will have their longing satisfied.

On the altar of a church in California stands a cross made of charred wood. Its material was once radioactive, for it was seared by the bomb that fell on Hiroshima. The wood was brought across the Pacific by a Japanese girl, who was injured in the blast and whose father was killed by it. Once radioactive, it is no longer so. The symbol of death has been formed into the symbol of life. If there can be such a transformation in the physical world, how much more can there be in us when God completes his work.

"We shall be changed." Death will end that acid of self-concern. Death will end the lack of love. Death will end this insecurity which threatens all joy. Death will end the weakness and faltering of our devotion. Death will end the infrequency of communion with God. Let us give thanks, for we shall be changed.

IN reporting what he had seen, and handled, and could no longer doubt, Paul said of the self: "It is sown a natural body, it is raised a spiritual body." Death is not like blowing out a match, for when you blow out a match, its usefulness is gone. Death is like planting a grain of wheat. What comes forth is something wonderfully different, and far more abundant than the hard grain folded into the earth, but still it is wheat. This all makes eminent good sense to those who know the resurrection of Christ.

Reinhold Niebuhr may have been the most influential thinker in America in this century. His Christian realism was rigorous and refreshing. He once observed that a certain article of faith was quite a stumbling block to his student generation. Those who employed it usually did so with a patronizing air toward the past. He writes: "Yet some of us have been persuaded to take the stone which we then rejected and make it the head of the corner. In other words, there is no part of the Apostolic creed which, in our present opinion, expresses the whole genius of the Christian faith more neatly than just this despised phrase: 'I believe in the resurrection of the body.'"

With Christ, we have a certainty, but not a blueprint. Center down in him, and not in your best hopes or your worst fears. Jesus did not say to the dying thief, "Buck up your courage, I hope we shall meet again." He said, "Today you will be with me in Paradise." That is so good a prospect as to make even the journey to him, death's little day, rather attractive.

F. PHILIPPOTAUX.

22

Worthy is the Lamb that was slain, and hath redeemed us to God by his blood, to receive power, and riches, and wisdom, and strength, and honour, and glory, and blessing.

Blessing and honour, glory and power, be unto him that sitteth upon the throne, and unto the Lamb, for ever and ever.

Amen.

WORTHY is the Lamb that was slain. The music is worthy of that text. Surely it ranks with the most powerful ever written. Try to hear in your depths this mighty chorus, with the measured cadence of that majestic opening. Then follows the stacatto building up of the tributes to Christ, like white clouds billowing up in a blue sky, piling ever higher and higher: "Power, and riches, and wisdom, and strength, and honour, and glory, and blessing." Glorious as are the words and music, they are but feeble efforts to say that Christ is worthy, and that all our unworthiness has been drowned in the overwhelming seas of the love of God. We love Christ because he first loved us. How theologically appropriate that *Messiah* usually closes with this soaring chorus of praise to the Lamb that was slain.

Worship is the soul's therapy. When you are sincerely praising and thanking God, you cannot be anxious about your self. Of course it is perfectly possible to go through religious observances perfunctorily, and never escape the bondage to self which you brought to the service. Trust Christ, and hold to him as the center, which is acceptable worship and the soul's way to health.

Hearing this final chorus, one is led closer to William Temple's view, which he expressed in a broadcast from England to the people of the United States. "I am disposed to begin by making what many people will feel to be a quite outrageous statement. This world can be saved from political chaos and collapse by one thing only and that is worship. For to worship is to quicken the conscience by the holiness of God, to feed the mind with the truth of God, to purge the imagination by the beauty of God, to open up the heart to the love of God, to devote the will to the purpose of God." Powerful claim! Those who have enthroned Christ know its validity.

OURS is not an age marked by a sense of the holy. Worship is scarcely the central activity of humanity in this day. The loss is immeasurable. T. S. Eliot captures the disintegration:

"Men have left God not for other gods,
    they say, but for no god; and this has
    never happened before
That men both deny gods and worship
    gods, professing first Reason,
And then Money, and Power, and what
    they call Life, or Race, or Dialectic . . .
In an age which advances progressively
    backwards . . .
When the church is no longer regarded,
    not even opposed, and men have
    forgotten
All gods except Usury, Lust and Power."

But this is Christmas, a pointing to the everlasting mercy, and to the wellsprings of renewal and glad fresh beginnings. The old carol reports reality: "Where meek souls will receive him, still the dear Christ enters in." He comes as light amid our darkness, as hope amid earth's hopelessness, and as eternal love amid the unloveliness of life. Does some mind stand off from Christ, finding it all slightly unreasonable? The New Testament reminds the learned: "All things were made by him; and without him was not any thing made that was made." There is reason's source, and to return to him is reason's finest choice. Does someone fear that this theology darkens life? Listen to Luther: "Christians are a blissful people, who can rejoice at heart and sing praises, stamp and dance and leap for joy. That is well pleasing to God, and doth our heart good, when we trust God and find in Him our pride and joyfulness."

IN the end, Christ himself is the vital argument for the faith. Some Christians make him winsome and attractive, others wear their faith as a hair shirt, slightly self-conscious, and at times decisively irritating. "Don't be put off by these gloomy caricatures of Christianity. For God's sake don't judge Jesus, the King of Joy, by them! Try the real thing—not that miserable parody of the reality—try the real thing, make friends with Jesus, stand where Peter and John and Andrew stood, and look into His eyes, listen to the music of His voice, answer His challenge, rise and follow, and you will find it the happiest life on earth." Christ is the living centre of it all, and to judge the faith by any other standard is simply unfair to the historical evidence.

If he had been born to privilege, lived in luxury, and died in like manner, he would have been long since forgotten. He came with an angel's song and a woman's cry of pain. Only of him do men write with rapture:

"Light looked down and beheld
        Darkness.
    'Thither will I go,' said Light.
Peace looked down and beheld War.
    'Thither will I go,' said Peace.
Love looked down and beheld Hatred.
    'Thither will I go,' said Love.
So came Light and shone.
So came Peace and gave rest.
So came Love and brought Life.
And the Word was made flesh, and dwelt
        among us."

His coming was so common. His life was so altogether lovely. His dying was redemptive. His rising was in power over death. His abiding is Emmanuel, God with us forever. "Worthy is the Lamb ..." Offer to him your soul's devotion, that he may reign in you, forever and ever.

APPENDIX I

RECITATIVE [TENOR]

Unto which of the angels said he at any time, Thou art my Son, this day have I begotten thee?

CHORUS

Let all the angels of God worship him.

AIR [BASS]

Thou art gone up on high, thou hast led captivity captive, and received gifts for men; yea, even for thine enemies, that the Lord God might dwell among them.

CHORUS

The Lord gave the word: great was the company of the preachers.

WE come now to those parts of *Messiah* which are seldom performed. In the Preface, we saw that Sir Thomas Beecham referred to them as being "on a lower inspirational level than the rest of the work." The text is scarcely more helpful than the music. We will do well to center our thought on two main passages. The first: "Thou art my Son, this day have I begotten thee." These words from the Second Psalm were immediately seized upon by the early church. In both Acts and Hebrews they are quoted as clear references to Christ. Those early Christians, witnessing as they were to a hostile world and to the Jewish community, wanted to show solid continuity between the age-old Scriptures and the new situation since Christ's coming. How better could they do it than simply to state that Christ was indeed the Son referred to in centuries of worship? Thus it is that when we refer to Christ as the Son of God, it is a title familiar in liturgy hundreds of years before he was born in Bethlehem.

The second striking passage is the natural outcome of the first, for whereas the title ascribed to Christ was central there, it is the work of Christ that is described in the phrase "Thou hast led captivity captive." When we think of the things that take us captive, hold our spirits back, and attempt to rob us of the confident faith he came to bring, then right over them all is this sign of Christ's accomplishment: "Thou hast led captivity captive."

Captivity to sin must be dealt with first, for sin is simply anything that separates us from God. Nothing is harder than to set the will against sin and expect to come off a victor. But if you set the figure of Christ before you, that very attractive sin loses its power. When Ulysses sailed past the isle of the Sirens, he had himself tied to the mast and the ears of his men stopped with wax, that they might not hear the Sirens singing. That is a picture of man's pitiful efforts to deal with sin in his own strength. But when Orpheus passed the same isle he could sit on deck, for he could make music more beautiful than that of the Sirens. The Christians strength in the face of sin is to say of Christ: "Thou has led this captivity captive." Such praise will deliver you wonderfully.

THE second captivity which Christ has dealt with is captivity to despair. The gloom is all around us. Almost any straight-line extrapolation from present practice would invite disastrous consequences. But is our day darker than the blackness on that hill outside Jerusalem on the first Good Friday? So thick was the gloom and so dispirited the disciples that they huddled together in an upper room for fear, and the only appropriate action was suggested by Peter—back to the fishing, and try to get over the disappointment that had shattered their dreams. It was into that hopeless situation that Christ returned, and led their despair captive by the sheer fact of his presence and his power.

No one can read the future, but the prophets of doom are holding forth everywhere. Quite realistically we must hold to the truth that the area of hope is still large. The newly released power may be used for beneficient purposes. Biological research just may rid the race of age-old diseases.

Food from the sea and power from the sun could well make food and energy more abundant than we have dared to dream. If Christians and their governments would become serious about feeding the world's hungry, they would surely find what has been clearly established—a higher standard of living is always followed by a reduction of the birth-rate. These human hopes have solid foundation.

Max Lerner once said he was not an optimist, or a pessimist, but a possibilist. That is a realistic stance. Yet the Christian knows a position even more realistic in dealing with the situation which is at once so threatening and so promising. The Christian goes deeper than either threats or promises. His confidence is not in himself, or in the best efforts of people, or in the brighter aspects of the human condition, but in the unchangeable love and inexhaustible mercy of God. Despair is not a Christian option. "Abandon the sole end for which I live, reject God's great commission and so die?" Browning's question was answered by the psalmist's promised Son, who led captivity captive and doomed only despair.

THE last captivity Christ led captive was what the New Testament so accurately calls the last enemy, death. Christmas could be a time for the soul's aching, if the season made us think backward only, a sad recalling of brighter days and happier times. We do remember those who made Christmas for us, and we remember not simply with nostalgia, but with sadness that they have passed from our sight. Right in the midst of such feelings we are to know that he who came at Advent defeated this last enemy. Christmas without Christ would be too much a looking back, a hurt summoning up Jeremiah's cry: "Why is my pain unceasing, my wound incurable, refusing to be healed?"

There came a day when Stopford Brooke looked back at the joys he had shared with his brother, now departed. In that mixture of sad remembrance and faith we all have known, he wrote: "I am . . . less liable to think of loss and more of gain when I consider the dead I have loved. I do not love them less, but even more. . . . They are with the highest Love; and William . . . will be crowded with enjoyment. It is a vast blessing . . . to be at rest about those who are gone from us and alive in God." There is a man who can honestly speak of his sense of loss, and yet have an even stronger sense that his loves are alive in God. Concerning our beloved dead we need to take Christ at his word: "My sheep hear my voice, and I know them, and they follow me: and I give unto them eternal life; and they shall never perish, neither shall any man pluck them out of my hand."

Our lives should be a daily witness that he who came at Advent has led captive the power of sin, and despair, and death. For that: "Let all the angels of God worship him" as we make a Christmas offering of our own praise and devotion.

APPENDIX II

RECITATIVE [CONTRALTO]

Then shall be brought to pass the saying that is written: Death is swallowed up in victory.

DUET [CONTRALTO AND TENOR]

O death, where is thy sting? O grave, where is thy victory?
The sting of death is sin, and the strength of sin is the law.

CHORUS

But thanks be to God, who giveth us the victory through our Lord Jesus Christ.

THIS shout of triumph is of the very essence of faith. It is indeed a cry of victory, not some weak statement of hope or vague optimism about the future. To some it will appear embarrassingly brazen, as though such complete spiritual health is unseemly. Even for many who believe quite firmly in the resurrection of Christ, the paean of praise never quite reaches this crescendo: "Thanks be to God, who giveth us the victory."

Why is our joy so low-keyed, and our sense of victory so muted? Surely it is because we have made ourselves the center of life's meaning, which is the place reserved for Christ in God's scheme of things. If we would daily recall that we belong to Christ, now and forever, we would not feel so threatened at the prospect of our own death. When we look steadily at a great light, we are not so conscious of the shadows round our feet, for the light is greater than the darkness. If we will rejoice more in the resurrection of Christ, then we will fear less about our own future.

Where is the true center? Is it in the self or in Christ? The difference is crucial, for it is the difference between anxiety and ultimate trust. A woman had several close friends die, then a dear member of her family was approaching the end of his life. She wrote: "It is hard for us to accept the fact that she may soon be leaving. If I am going to constantly meet this unspeakable terror in friend after friend, I shall have to either trust more in God or reserve a room in Norristown [the mental hospital]." That is accurate. We should be living down to the unspeakable terror, as she calls death, or living up to that triumphant level where faith vibrates with the resurrection of Christ. "Thanks be to God, who giveth us the victory through our Lord Jesus Christ."

THE light touch, even a hint of humor, is sometimes helpful in grasping truth. It is so with the New Testament expression: "the resurrection of the body." Someone is sure to stumble over that and think it means a continuation of Aunt Mary's arthritis or the eternal necessity of bifocals. William Temple is very helpful at this point. He was one of the intellectual giants of this century. In his own right he was a ranking philosopher, a first-rate interpreter and expositor of Plato. He became Archbishop of Canterbury, the highest post in the Church of England. Temple had prepped at Rugby and on the occasion of the reunion of his class he arranged for the old grads to meet in a small town at the foot of a mountain. After lunch they all set off to hike to the top. Temple arrived last, puffing and blowing, perhaps the paunchiest of them all. Fixing the group with the eye of an archbishop, he said, "Thank God, gentlemen, we do not believe in the resurrection of the flesh."

It isn't the death of friends in their later years that should make us sad and depressed. Friends who die in Christ are destined for a living and self-enhancing experience. What should depress us is to meet an old school friend or former associate, who, instead of maturing in faith, with a deepening sense of the spiritual, has simply stiffened and become more stolid. That is loss indeed.

Here is a poem entitled "Pre-Valedictory," apt way of viewing death. Humor, trust, and beauty are all expressed in this faith.

> ". . . by the Eternal, I am not
>   expendable. . . .
> Take heed to St. Paul, and do not ask
> 'With what manner of body . . . ?'
> Why, I wouldn't be caught dead with a
>   body.
>   Should you care to note my withdrawal
> In the manner that best links spirit and
>   matter,
>   Play the Emperor Concerto, second
>   movement, and Disperse, but
>   cheerfully."

CHRISTIANS should take God at his word: "Then shall be brought to pass the saying that is written: Death is swallowed up in victory." It was written for you. It is how you are to contemplate your own earthly end and your new beginning. Of course the last enemy is death, bitter death. And the worst sting is that of the grave, the slow yielding of some dear body to the earth. But it is precisely that sting, and that bitterness which has been transmuted into light, and love, and immortality, through the gospel, which gospel rests squarely on resurrection faith.

When you consider the dead whom you have loved, you are really considering the living, for whom Christ died and rose again. The ache of their absence from us is very sore, but could we wish them back? Yes, we could wish them back, but it would be to add to our life, for it would not enhance theirs who are already in the Presence and in the Light. Rather than looking back and recalling those dear days which once we knew, the soul should live each day forward, to where they are, and where we are all soon to follow, praising and thanking God. Make the resurrection of Christ the center of your universe:

"He knows the way to come and go—
Comes with a star, goes with a cross,
And comes again with a triumph;
He is risen."

Handel's last public appearance was on Good Friday, 1759. The occasion—a performance of *Messiah*. At its conclusion he collapsed. Regaining consciousness, he said: "I want to die on Good Friday, in the hope of rejoining the good God, my sweet Lord and Saviour, on the day of his Resurrection." That wish was granted. May our end here be like his.

APPENDIX III

If God be for us, who can be against us?
Who shall lay any thing to the charge of
God's elect?
It is God that justifieth.
Who is he that condemneth?

It is Christ that died, yea, rather, that is
risen again, who is at the right hand of
God, who makes intercession for us.

IF God be for us, who can be against us? We may concur with Sir Thomas Beecham's judgment that the music to accompany this text does not rank in quality with the familiar portions of the oratorio, and that is reason enough for it to be omitted in modern performances of *Messiah*. But to omit this text, and its setting in the book of Romans, from the faith, would be loss irreparable. Romans is crucial to Paul's thought, the pivotal point in Augustine's conversion, the rock foundation of Luther, and the standing ground for Barth and Bonhoeffer in the twentieth century. The passage immediately following this text in the eighth chapter reads: "Who shall separate us from the love of Christ? Shall tribulation, or distress, or persecution, or famine, or nakedness, or peril or sword? . . . No, in all these things we are more than conquerors through him who loved us."

Concerning these passages, Paul Tillich wrote: "These words are among the most powerful ever written. Their sound is able to grasp human souls in desperate situations. In my own experience they have proved to be stronger than the sound of exploding shells, of weeping at open graves, of the sighs of the sick, of the moaning of the dying. They are stronger than the self-accusation of those who are in despair about themselves and they prevail over the permanent whisper of anxiety in the depth of our being."

Both eminent theologian and the most untutored among us can be grasped by this clear word. "If God be for us, who can be against us?" And immediately afterward **Messiah** carries us forward to Christ: "that died, yea, rather, that is risen again." Nothing shall be able to separate us from him. Saint Teresa, when told she would soon die, exclaimed: "O my Lord, my Lord, the longed-for hour has come, the hour in which I shall see Thee! The good time which I welcome, the hour when I must leave my exile and my soul shall enjoy the fulfillment of all her desire."

GOD intended us to live in that strong certainty, but we have allowed reason, God's best gift after love, to cloud our confidence. We have allowed our searching minds in the natural world to become skeptical minds concerning any ultimate meaning. Von Weizsäcker, the scientist who was the first to propose a detailed system of nuclear reactions to account for the source of energy in the sun and stars, and who firmly established the nebular theory of the evolution of our planetary system, defines the situation: "Scepticism has been the privilege of a few men of learning who could survive because around them stood a world of faith unshaken. Today, scepticism has entered the masses, and has rocked the foundations of their order of life. It is the men of learning who are frightened now." And again he writes: "It is an old saying that the first sip from the cup of knowledge cuts us off from God—but in the bottom of the cup God waits for those who seek him. . . . Love can be given to us—that is the whole substance of the Christian doctrine of salvation. It is rarely given to us before, in despair of ourselves, we have asked for it."

Ask for the gift at Christmas. Ask longingly of a loving God, and he will give you the best gift of all. That gift is faith in God, through Jesus Christ, our Lord. If you have received so much, but still stand with an empty heart, ask for that gift. If you have learned so much, but have not learned of him, ask for that gift. If you have found life to be without meaning, and want to believe that there is purpose behind the whole cosmic process, ask for that gift. If you have thought yourself to count for nothing in the vast eras of time and the immensities of space, remember you are a person for whom Christ came and for whom he died. How dare you think little of yourself, since Christ came into the world at Christmas for you. Remember that, and lift up your head.

CHRISTMAS is the time for returning in memory to places and persons once dear and central in our lives. Yet all places and persons are temporal and passing. Now is the time to return to the faith, dear and central to all who have welcomed the coming of Christ. Those who saw him when the word became flesh became Christ-centered persons. We are invited to that same relationship. They lived by the good news of One who had been born of a woman even as we were, lived our common life, endured its troubles, and was in all points tempted such as we are, yet he did not sin. He was crucified, died, and buried, arose from the dead, and now lives, quick to help, and mighty to save. By faith in him, we are to live, and die.

At Christmas, renew the relationship with him. Let the day of his birth be the day of your rebirth into the deepest faith of all. God offers this gift of Christ at Christmas. Simply say in the words of the marraige service: "O living Christ, I pledge myself to you; in plenty and in want; in joy and in sorrow; in sickness and in health; as long as we both shall live." That will be for eternity.

This is not your own doing, your own strength, your own goodness at work. That would be too flimsy a foundation. You are responding to One who first came to you, invited you, and offered you the gift of meaning and love. Though all the world conspire to shake you, now you know: "If God be for us, who can be against us?"

Join that multitude in the first century when he came, and in every century since, in love and praise: "Unto him who is able to keep you from falling, and to present you faultless before the presence of his glory with exceeding joy, to the only wise God, our Saviour, be glory and majesty, dominion and power, both now and ever." Amen.

References

In this volume, texts from the Bible in Handel's *Messiah* and quotations from other sources are listed in the order of their use.

Preface

Sir Thomas Beecham, in an essay entitled "Handel's Messiah," written to accompany a recorded performance. 1959.

From Sir Thomas Beecham's autobiography, *A Mingled Chime* (G. P. Putnam's Sons, Inc., 1943).

1
Isaiah 40:1–3

"Let me no more my comfort draw," from hymn by John Campbell Shairp.

2
Isaiah 40:4–5

"As I prepare," Siegmund A. E. Betz, *The Pulpit*, December 1955.

3

Haggai 2:6–7; Malachi 3:1–3.

From William Temple, *Christ's Revelation of God*, quoted in *William Temple's Teaching*, ed. by A. E. Baker (The Westminster Press, 1951), p. 63.

4

Isaiah 7:14

"He has given us the sun," from Sigrid Undset, *Christmas and Twelfth Night* (Longmans, Green & Co., 1932), pp. 39f.

5

Isaiah 40:9; 60:1

T. S. Eliot, from "Choruses from 'The Rock,'" *Collected Poems, 1909–1962* (Harcourt, Brace & World, Inc., 1963; Faber & Faber, Ltd., 1963), p. 163. Used by permission.

"O God, I offer thee my heart," from "Religion and Common Sense," by Gerald Watkins, in *The Pulpit*, January 1966, p. 6.

"Light of the world," from hymn by Horatius Bonar.

"It is a duty we owe to God," from John Locke, *Essay Concerning Human Understanding*.

6
Isaiah 60:2–3.

"Come not in darkness," William Sidney Walker (1795–1846).
"The great world's altar-stairs," from "In Memoriam," LV, stanza 4, Alfred Lord Tennyson.
"Holding festival . . . in our whole life," quoted in *The Interpreter's Bible*, Vol. 5, pp. 698f.
"That one Face," from *Dramatis Personae* epilogue, 3d speaker xii, Robert Browning.

7
Isaiah 9:2, 6.

Boris Pasternak, *Doctor Zhivago* (Pantheon Books, Inc., 1958), p. 43.
William Temple, quoted by Leslie D. Weatherhead, *Over His Own Signature* (Abingdon Press, 1956), p. 51.
"Only the road," from "The Seekers," John Masefield.

8
Luke 2:8–11.

Inscription in Elton Trueblood, *The Common Ventures of Life* (Harper & Brothers, Publishers, 1965), p. 102.

"To an open house in the evening," G. K. Chesterton, quoted by Miles Lowell Yates, *The King in His Beauty* (The Seabury Press, Inc., 1957), p. 29.

9
Luke 2:13–14.

"Gather us in," from hymn by George Matheson.

"Thou art smitten," from "The Hymn of Man," Algernon Charles Swinburne.

10
Zechariah 9:9–10; Isaiah 35:5–6.

11
Isaiah 40:11; Matthew 11:28–30.

"As the marsh-hen," from "The Marshes of Glynn," Sidney Lanier.

"One thing strikes my heart with terror," Victor Hugo.

"And I smiled to think God's greatness,"
Elizabeth Barrett Browning, "Rhyme of
the Duchess May," Conclusion, Stanza
II.

"O blessed burden," from hymn by Bernard
of Clairvaux.

"O Love that wilt not let me go," from
hymn by George Matheson.

12

John 1:29; Isaiah 53:3.

"Nothing in my hand I bring," from the
hymn "Rock of Ages," by Augustus
Montague Toplady.

Dietrich Bonhoeffer, *The Cost of Discipleship* (SCM Press, Ltd., 1948), pp. 38
–39.

"To say that God is love," William Temple,
Palm Sunday to Easter, quoted in *William
Temple's Teaching*, ed. by A. E. Baker,
p. 82.

13

Isaiah 53:4–6.

"I watched her in the loud and shadowy
lanes," sonnet ascribed to Mary Webb.

Quoted in *The Interpreter's Bible*, Vol. 5, p. 623.

"If we have never sought, we seek Thee now," from the poem "Jesus of the Scars," Edward Shillito, in *Five Minutes a Day*, by Robert E. Speer (The Westminster Press, 1943), p. 355.

14
Psalm 22:7–8; 69:20.

"I found him nearest," from hymn by George Macdonald.
"Reality, reality," William Stidger.

15
Lamentations 1:12; Isaiah 53:8; Psalm 16:10.

"Friend, it is over now," from "Good Friday," John Masefield.
"Judge not the Play," Francis Quarles, quoted by George Shaw Stewart, *Lower Levels of Prayer* (SCM Press, Ltd., 1939), p. 179.

16
Psalm 24:7–10.

"Lift up your heads, ye mighty gates," from hymn by George Weissel, tr. by Catherine Winkworth.

17
Isaiah 52:7; Romans 10:18 (Psalm 19:4).

Bishop Azariah, quoted from *Pulpit Digest*, January 22, 1954.

U.S. ambassador to the UN, quoted from *The Christian Century*, October 9, 1957.

Alfred North Whitehead, *Science and the Modern World* (The Macmillan Company, 1925), pp. 275–276.

Henry van Dyke, *The Other Wise Man*.

"O Zion, haste," from the hymn by Mary Ann Thomson.

18
Psalm 2:1–4, 9.

"Between the wrath of God," James S. Stewart, *A Man in Christ* (Harper & Brothers, Publishers, 1935), p. 219.

"She set a rose to blossom in her hair," poem by Rabelais, cited in Harry Emerson Fosdick, *On Being a Real Person* (Harper & Brothers, Publishers, 1943), p. 241.

"Men may have to wait long," in *The Interpreter's Bible*, Vol. 4, p. 25.

Martin Niemoeller, quoted by Halford Luccock, *The Acts of the Apostles* (Willett, Clark & Company, 1942), p. 84.

19
Revelation 19:6; 11:15; 19:16.

"The high that proved too high," from "Abt Vogler," Robert Browning.

"Things fall apart," from "The Second Coming," William Butler Yeats.

"This is clearly the promise," J. Brandt McCabe, personal letter to the author, paraphrasing an unknown source.

20
Job 19:25–26; I Corinthians 15:20.

"Call me not dead," Richard Watson Gilder (altered), quoted by Robert E. Speer, in *Five Minutes a Day*, p. 174.

"Some day the bell will sound," from "School Days," Maltie D. Babcock.

"When I die," author unknown.

21

I Corinthians 15:21–22, 51–52.

Ruskin, quoted by Arthur John Gossip, *The Hero in Thy Soul* (Charles Scribner's Sons, 1933), pp. 168–169.

Reinhold Niebuhr, *Beyond Tragedy* (Charles Scribner's Sons, 1937), p. 290.

22

Revelation 5:12–13.

William Temple, *The Hope of a New World* (The Macmillan Company, 1941).

T. S. Eliot, from "Choruses from 'The Rock,'" *Collected Poems, 1909–1962*, p. 164. Used by permission.

"Where meek souls will receive him," from Phillips Brooks's carol, "O Little Town of Bethlehem."

Martin Luther, sermon preached October 18, 1529.

"Don't be put off," James S. Stewart, *The Gates of New Life* (Charles Scribner's Sons, 1938), p. 23.

"Light looked down," Laurence Housman, in *Masterpieces of Religious Verse*, ed. by James D. Morrison (Harper & Brothers, Publishers, 1948), No. 423.

Appendix I
Hebrews 1:5–6; Psalm 68:18, 11.

"I am . . . less liable to think of loss," Stopford Brooke, quoted by W. Robertson Nicoll, *Reunion in Eternity* (George H. Doran Company, 1919), p. 178.

Appendix II
I Corinthians 15:54–56.

"It is hard for us," from a personal letter to the author.

"By the Eternal," Donald C. Babcock, in *Atlantic*, January 1951. Copyright © 1950, by The Atlantic Monthly Company, Boston, Mass.

"He knows the way to come and go," John R. Slater, "An Easter Reveille," quoted by David MacLennan, *Joyous Adventure* (Harper & Brothers, Publishers, 1952), p. 122.

Appendix III
Paul Tillich, *The New Being* (Charles Scribner's Sons, 1955), p. 50.
C. F. von Weizsäcker, *The History of*

Nature (The University of Chicago Press, 1949), pp. 177–188.

THE END

Large Print Inspirational Books from Walker

Would you like to be on our Large Print mailing list?
Please send your name and address to:

B. Walker
Walker and Company
720 Fifth Avenue
New York, NY 10019

Among available titles are:

The Prophet
Kahlil Gibran

Gift from the Sea
Ann Morrow Lindbergh

The Power of Positive Thinking
Norman Vincent Peale

Words to Love by
Mother Teresa

A Gathering of Hope
Helen Hayes

Woman to Woman
Eugenia Price

The Burden is Light
Eugenia Price

Apples of Gold
Jo Petty

Getting Through the Night: Finding Your
Way After the Loss of a Loved One
Eugenia Price

The Genesee Diary:
Report from a
Trappist Monastery
Henri J. M. Nouwen

God in the Hard Times
Dale Evans Rogers

A Grief Observed
C. S. Lewis

He Began with Eve
Joyce Landorf

Hinds' Feet on High Places
Hannah Hurnard

Hope and Faith for Tough Times
Robert H. Schuller

Irregular People
Joyce Landorf

Jonathan Livingston Seagull
Richard Bach

The Little Flowers of Saint Francis of Assisi
Illustrated with woodcuts

No Man Is an Island
Thomas Merton

Reflections on the Pslams
C. S. Lewis

The Road Less Traveled: A New Psychology of Love, Traditional Values and Spiritual Growth
M. Scott Peck, M.D.

The Sacred Journey
Frederick Buechner

The Secret Kingdom
Pat Robertson

The Seven Storey Mountain
Thomas Merton

Surprised by Joy
The Shape of My Early Life
C. S. Lewis

Something Beautiful for God:
Mother
Teresa of Calcutta
Malcolm Muggeridge

Not I, But Christ
Corrie ten Boom

Out of Solitude
Henri J. M. Nouwen

Peace With God
Billy Graham

The Practice of the Presence of God
Brother Lawrence
Introduction by Dorothy Day

Prayers and Promises for Every Day
From the Living Bible
with Corrie Ten Boom

Reaching Out
Henri J. M. Nouwen

Abraham Lincoln: A Spiritual Biography
Elton Trueblood

The Day Christ Was Born
Jim Bishop

Enjoy the Lord
Father John Catoir

God Cares for You
Richard Dayringer

Golden Treasury of Psalms and Prayers
Selected by Edna Beilenson

Handel's Messiah: A Devotional Commentary
Joseph McCabe

The Life of the Soul
Samuel Miller

Teach Me to Pray
Gabe Huck

When the Well Runs Dry
Thomas H. Green, S.J.

The Adventure of Spiritual Healing
Michael Drury

The Alphabet of Grace
Frederick Buechner

A Book of Hours
Elizabeth Yates

Beginning to Pray
Anthony Bloom

A Certain Life: Contemporary Meditations
on the Way of Christ
Herbert O'Driscoll

The Christian Faith
David H. C. Read

A Diary of Private Prayer
John Baillie

Fear No Evil
David Watson

God at Eventide
by A. J. Russell

A Guide to Christian Meditation
Marilyn Morgan Helleberg

Inner Healing: God's Great Assurance
Theodore E. Dobson

Instrument of Thy Peace
Alan Paton

Introducing the Bible
William Barclay

The Irrational Season
Madeleine L'Engle

Living Simply Through the Day
Tilden Edwards

The Master's Men: Character Sketches of
the Disciples
William Barclay

Opening to God
Thomas H. Green, S.J.

Prayer and Personal Religion
John B. Coburn

The Pursuit of Holiness
Jerry Bridges

Sea Edge
W. Phillip Keller

The Touch of the Earth
Jean Hersey

To God be the Glory
Edited by Roger Elwood

To Help You Through the Hurting
Marjorie Holmes

Up From Grief
Bernadine Kreis
Alice Pattie

Walking With Loneliness
Paula Ripple

The Way of the Wolf
Martin Bell

Who Will Deliver Us? The Present Power
of the Death of Christ
Paul F.M. Zahl

The Will of God
Leslie D. Weatherhead

Your God Is Too Small
J. B. Phillips

Emotions: Can You Trust Them
Dr. James Dodson

The Four Loves
C. S. Lewis

The Greatest Salesman in the World
Og Mandino

The Guideposts Christmas Treasury
Editors of Guideposts

The Healing Light
Agnes Sanford

Healing Prayer
Barbara Leahy Shlemon

Making All Things New
Henri J. M. Nouwen

More Than a Carpenter
Josh McDowell

Spirit-Controlled Temperament
Tim LaHaye

Wings of Silver
Jo Petty

Strength to Love
Martin Luther King, Jr.

**A Time For Remembering
The Ruth Bell Graham Story**
Patricia Daniels Cornwell

Three Steps Forward, Two Steps Back
Charles R. Swindoll

**The True Joy of Positive Living
An Autobiography**
Norman Vincent Peale

With Open Hands
Henri J. M. Nouwen